Toussaint L

C000259871

Revolutionary Lives

Series Editors: Sarah Irving, University of Edinburgh;
Professor Paul Le Blanc, La Roche College, Pittsburgh

Revolutionary Lives is a series of short, critical biographies of radical figures from throughout history. The books are sympathetic but not sycophantic, and the intention is to present a balanced and, where necessary, critical evaluation of the individual's place in their political field, putting their actions and achievements in context and exploring issues raised by their lives, such as the use or rejection of violence, nationalism, or gender in political activism. While individuals are the subject of the books, their personal lives are dealt with lightly except insofar as they mesh with political concerns. The focus is on the contribution these revolutionaries made to history, an examination of how far they achieved their aims in improving the lives of the oppressed and exploited, and how they can continue to be an inspiration for many today.

Also available:

Toussaint Louverture

A Black Jacobin in the Age of Revolutions

Charles Forsdick and Christian Høgsbjerg

PlutoPress
www.plutobooks.com

First published 2017 by Pluto Press
345 Archway Road, London N6 5AA

www.plutobooks.com

Copyright © Charles Forsdick and Christian Høgsbjerg 2017

The right of Charles Forsdick and Christian Høgsbjerg to be identified as
the authors of this work has been asserted by them in accordance with the
Copyright, Designs and Patents Act 1988.

British Library Cataloguing in Publication Data
A catalogue record for this book is available from the British Library

ISBN   978 0 7453 3515 5   Hardback
ISBN   978 0 7453 3514 8   Paperback
ISBN   978 1 7868 0028 2   PDF eBook
ISBN   978 1 7868 0030 5   Kindle eBook
ISBN   978 1 7868 0029 9   EPUB eBook

This book is printed on paper suitable for recycling and made from fully managed
and sustained forest sources. Logging, pulping and manufacturing processes are
expected to conform to the environmental standards of the country of origin.

Typeset by Stanford DTP Services, Northampton, England

Simultaneously printed in the United Kingdom and United States of America

For Robert A. Hill and Janet Alder

Contents

Illustrations

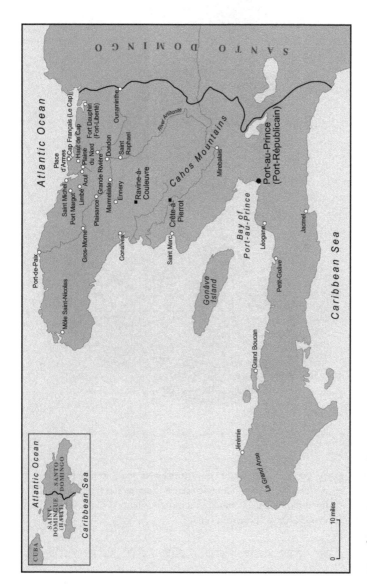

Map of Saint-Domingue/Haiti.

Frontispiece: Portrait of Toussaint Louverture by Nicolas Eustache Maurin.
From *Iconographie des contemporains depuis 1789 jusqu'à 1829* (Paris, 1838).
Clark Art Institute, Williamstown, Massachusetts. Courtesy of the John
Carter Brown Library at Brown University.

Acknowledgements

Our debts in writing this popular biography of Toussaint Louverture are first and foremost to those many historians of the Haitian Revolution upon whose collective labour this volume rests, though we of course take responsibility for any errors remaining and for the specific interpretation and arguments advanced. As will soon be apparent, we owe our major debt of gratitude here to C.L.R. James, and we have both recently had the great honour of editing *The Black Jacobins Reader* for the C.L.R. James Archives series with Duke University Press. We therefore felt it was only right to dedicate this work to the Jamaican historian Robert A. Hill, who as editor of that series not only generously entrusted us with *The Black Jacobins Reader* project but also gave us kind support and expert guidance throughout. Robert's outstanding scholarship on the African diaspora in general and Caribbean radicals like Marcus Garvey and C.L.R. James in particular remains an inspiration. We would also like to dedicate the work to another inspiring figure, Janet Alder, whose tireless campaigning for justice for her brother Christopher, who died in police custody in Hull in 1998, is just one of many contemporary struggles to make 'Black Lives Matter'. As Hull celebrates being UK City of Culture in 2017, much will be made no doubt of the abolitionist campaigning of local MP William Wilberforce, but one day the story of Janet Alder's now 20-year-long struggle to try and uncover the truth about what happened to Christopher Alder will surely be recognised as just as important and significant a part of that city's history.

Thanks are also due to Talat Ahmed, Ian Birchall, Roger Norman Buckley, Margaret Busby, Pablo Butcher, Édouard Duval Carrié, François Cauvin, David Clayton, Kimathi Donkor, Lubaina Himid, Martin Hoyles, Peter James Hudson (and his superb website, *The Public Archive: Black History in Dark Times*), Margaret Kane, Charlot Lucien, Graham Mustin, Bill Schwarz, Ulrick Jean-Pierre and Robin Urquhart. Alan Forrest deserves special thanks for kindly reading and commenting on the manuscript in draft. We would also like to thank the staff of the British Library, John Carter Brown Library, Leeds University Library and McGill University Library. This chapter was written while Charles Forsdick was AHRC Theme Leadership Fellow for 'Translating Cultures' (AH/N504476/1). He records his gratitude for this support. Finally, we would like to thank Jonathan Maunder for suggesting this biography in the first place, the editors of the 'Revolutionary Lives' series and their anonymous readers, and David Castle, Melanie Patrick, Robert Webb and the whole team at Pluto Press for their patience, support and fine work with this publication.

Introduction

Haiti is the country where Negro people stood up for the first time, affirming their determination to shape a world, a free world . . . Haiti represented for me the heroic Antilles, the African Antilles . . . Haiti is the most African of the Antilles. It is at the same time a country with a marvellous history: the first Negro epic of the New World was written by Haitians, people like Toussaint Louverture, Henri Christophe, Jean-Jacques Dessalines.

So declared the great Martinican poet and activist Aimé Césaire in a 1967 interview with the Haitian poet René Depestre, stressing the inspiration for him of the Haitian Revolution of 1791–1804, a set of events that led to the birth of the world's first independent black republic outside Africa.[1] Césaire's classic anti-colonialist 1939 poem *Notebook of a Return to My Native Land* was a founding poetic text of *Négritude* – a movement which influenced Depestre himself. It also contained a powerful tribute to the tragic heroic leader of the Haitian Revolution, Toussaint Louverture, evoking his period of imprisonment in the French Jura mountains at the hands of First Consul Napoleon Bonaparte and linking this to a more general experience of 'blackness':

What is mine too: a small cell in the Jura,
The snow lines it with white bars
The snow is a white gaoler who mounts guard in front of a prison
What is mine
a man alone, imprisoned by whiteness
a man alone who defies the white screams of a white death
(TOUSSAINT, TOUSSAINT LOUVERTURE)[2]

From William Wordsworth's mournful sonnet 'To Toussaint Louverture', written in the year of Toussaint's arrest in 1802, up to musicians such as Sidney Bechet, Santana, Wyclef Jean, Charles Mingus and Courtney Pine, the Haitian Revolution has, as Philip Kaisary recently noted, generated an 'extraordinary and voluminous cultural archive' as 'a diverse array of writers, artists and intellectuals' were fascinated by an epic liberation struggle that 'overthrew slavery, white supremacy and colonialism'.[3] It was truly a world-historic event, but until the last couple of decades or so has tended historically to be overlooked or 'silenced' by historians outside Haiti itself.[4] The late Haitian scholar Michel-Rolph Trouillot in 1995 noted its 'unthinkability' to prevailing classical Eurocentric modes of thought, by which he signified the fact that 'the Haitian Revolution thus entered history with the peculiar characteristic of being unthinkable even as it happened.'[5]

As Césaire noted, it was in Haiti that the 'colonial problem' was first posed in all its complexity.[6] In 1492, the tropical Caribbean island was 'discovered' for the Spanish Empire by Christopher Columbus, an encounter that resulted in the half-a-million strong existing indigenous Taino population being all but exterminated within a generation as a ruthless search for rivers of gold led only to rivers of blood. Columbus had described 'Ayiti', as the Taino had called it ('Land of mountains'), as a 'paradise', and promptly therefore renamed the island 'La Espanola' – or Hispaniola – 'Little Spain'. For the Taino, however, their hopes of finding paradise were irredeemably lost. While the knot of colonialism may have been first tied in Haiti, Césaire also noted that the subsequent generations of Haitians were also one of the very first peoples to untie it, for the Haitian Revolution, which culminated in Haiti's declaration of independence on New Year's Day 1804, saw the birth of one of the world's first post-colonial nations. It is only if one has some appreciation of the world-historical importance and inspiration of the Haitian Revolution that one can begin to understand why Western imperial powers have tied a tight neo-colonial noose around Haiti ever since.[7]

The Black Jacobins and the Role of the Individual in History

The magisterial work that arguably for the first time elevated the Haitian Revolution to its rightful place in modern world history was *The Black Jacobins: Toussaint Louverture and the San Domingo Revolution* by the Trinidadian Marxist historian Cyril Lionel Robert James, first published in 1938. C.L.R. James was of course more than just the author of *The Black Jacobins*; a towering Pan-Africanist intellectual and activist, he was also a pioneer of the modern West Indian novel, a literary critic, playwright, sports writer and one of the twentieth century's outstanding representatives of the revolutionary democratic tradition of 'socialism from below'.[8] *The Black Jacobins*, one of the grandest of 'grand narratives' ever penned, stands as perhaps James's *magnum opus*. It has long won for itself the status of a classic, and not simply among Marxists. Though there have been some outstanding accounts of the Haitian Revolution written since 1938, including perhaps most notably Laurent Dubois's *Avengers of the New World* (2004), *The Black Jacobins* not only – as the historian James Walvin has noted – 'remains *the* pre-eminent account' of the Haitian Revolution, 'despite the vast accumulation of detail and argument advanced by armies of scholars' since, but also stands as the ideal 'starting point' for understanding the experience of slavery in general.[9]

In his preface to *The Black Jacobins*, C.L.R. James famously noted how the Haitian Revolution is 'the only successful slave revolt in history, and the odds it had to overcome is evidence of the magnitude of the interests that were involved'. He continued:

The transformation of slaves, trembling in hundreds before a single white man, into a people able to organise themselves and defeat the most powerful European nations of their day, is one of the great epics of revolutionary struggle and achievement . . . by a phenomenon often observed, the individual leadership responsible for this unique achievement was almost entirely the work of a single man – Toussaint Louverture . . . between 1789 and 1815, with the single exception of Bonaparte himself, no single figure appeared on the historical stage more greatly gifted . . . yet Toussaint did not make the revolution. It was the revolution that made Toussaint. And even that is not the whole truth.[10]

3

Louverture has now been the subject of extensive biographical attention across two centuries, ranging from largely denigratory accounts of his life published while he was still alive (by authors such as Cousin d'Avalon and Dubroca), to much more recent and carefully researched accounts by Madison Smartt Bell, Jean-Louis Donnadieu and Philippe Girard. All biographers, faced with significant gaps in the archive regarding Louverture's life prior to the outbreak of the Haitian Revolution in 1791, are obliged nevertheless to address how a man born into slavery in the 1740s managed, five decades later, to mastermind resistance against the French, British and Spanish, to deliver emancipation from slavery, and to lay the foundations for what would be the second independent state in the Americas. The Victorian writer Thomas Carlyle had stated in his famous 1841 Lectures 'On Heroes, Hero-Worship and the Heroic in History' that for him:

> Universal History, the history of what man has accomplished in the world, is at bottom the History of the Great Men who have worked here . . . the leaders of men . . . the modellers, patterns, and in wide sense the creators, of whatsoever the general mass of men contrived to do or to attain . . . the History of the World . . . was the Biography of Great Men.[11]

Even though Carlyle, himself a notorious racist, would not have felt Toussaint Louverture worthy of the title of a 'Great Man' – indeed he regarded Louverture as 'a murderous Three-fingered Jack' – the insistence by many biographers on Louverture's exceptionalism has, unwittingly or otherwise, reflected such a logic.[12]

James's *Black Jacobins*, in identifying the revolutionary leader in its subtitle, struggles with these issues, with its author claiming of his protagonist at one point that though 'we have clearly stated the vast impersonal forces at work in the crisis of San Domingo . . . men make history, and Toussaint made the history that he made because he was the man he was'.[13] Though James always qualified and disciplined his judgements on Louverture with reference to the concrete historical context, he clearly wanted to vindicate Louverture's achievements in the context of racist portrayals from the likes of Carlyle as well as register the critical role Louverture's individual leadership played in shaping the Haitian Revolution throughout the work:

> At a certain stage, the middle of 1794, the potentialities in the chaos began to be shaped and soldered by his powerful personality, and thenceforth it is impossible to say where the social forces end and the impress of personality begins. It is sufficient that but for him this history would be entirely different.[14]

James, however, progressively adjusted his own views on the balance between historiography and biography over the course of his life to the extent that – in a series of lectures at the Institute of the Black World in Atlanta in 1971 – he explored a new approach in which Louverture would be, if not totally eclipsed, at least no longer placed centre-stage in a rewriting of the Haitian Revolution 'from below'.[15]

The Mythologisation of Louverture

Those attempting to understand Louverture's life are not only faced with archival gaps, but also forced to negotiate the extensive mythologisation by which these have been filled. As one early biographer, Percy Waxman, once noted, 'so much that is purely legendary has been written about Toussaint Louverture and so little trustworthy "source material" exists that it is extremely difficult for one with no gift for fiction to attempt a complete story of his life'.[16]

Mythmaking about Louverture is not only, however, a case of fiction filling the vacuum left by this lack of archival traces. As recent new research on the Haitian Revolution by scholars such as David Geggus and Philippe Girard has shown, despite the paucity of information before 1791, there is a rich body of material in English, French and Spanish that covers the years of the Revolution itself as well as the War of Independence leading to the establishment of Haiti in January 1804.[17] The mythologisation of Louverture began during his lifetime, with biographies and various eyewitness accounts of him serving to praise and condemn him in equal measure, according to the ideological stance of their authors. A central aspect of many of these narratives was speculation on the revolutionary's origins, in an attempt – by his detractors – to explain the origins of his violence and deceit, or – by his apologists – to underline the exceptional circumstances that led to his emergence as a leader.

Deborah Jenson has suggested that Louverture contributed to these processes himself by acting as his own spin-doctor, and it is clear that through a carefully orchestrated engagement with the international press, as well as the drafting of his memoir during the final months of his life, the revolutionary leader sought to craft his biographical narratives whilst shaping his own posthumous reputation.[18] In a recent article drawing on archival sources to test many of the received versions of Toussaint's life before the Revolution, Philippe Girard and Jean-Louis Donnadieu describe this process when they claim:

> When reminiscing about his past, Toussaint was walking a fine line: he had to portray himself as a faithful slave to appeal to conservative planters, underline his long-standing admiration for Raynal to appeal to French republicans, emphasise his past as a slave rebel to maintain his credibility with the black rank and file, and offer a narrative of piety, fidelity, and obedience to set an example for the field laborers who were balking at his attempt to revive the plantation system. Toussaint, who liked to be described as a black Spartacus and was conscious of his historical importance, may also have massaged his past with an eye to his standing among future generations.[19]

Mindful of this context, David Bell has recently asked: 'Will there ever be a truly authoritative biography of Toussaint Louverture?', to which – in the light of archival lacunae and the contradictory detail often circulating as fact – he replies: 'Unfortunately, the answer is probably no'.[20] Although mythologization is not exclusive in any way to Louverture himself (Napoleon – despite no shortage of archival material and the existence of many authoritative biographies – was and remains subject to similar processes of mythologisation), the slippage between historical phenomenon and politico-cultural legend is accordingly marked, and serves as a fascinating subject of enquiry in its own right.[21]

In one of the most useful anthologies of the extensive catalogue of posthumous re-figurings of Louverture, George Tyson states: 'he has been all things to all men, from bloodthirsty black savage to "the greatest black man in history"'.[22] What is of interest is, precisely, the often contradictory complexity of this mythologisation or instrumentalisation, i.e. the ways in which the context of production of versions of Louverture impact on these diverse posthumous re-figurings, creating often unexpected connections between the Haitian revolutionary and other distinct historico-political moments and cultural settings. For aspects of the revolutionary's life from the years following the outbreak of the revolution, as the variable interpretations of Louverture's trajectory make amply clear, negotiating the evidence can be a matter of ideological choice, with certain biographers – such as Pierre Pluchon – seeking to domesticate the revolutionary implications of their subject's history and present him even as an *ancien régime* figure.[23]

The New Conservative Revisionism

Such a strand of thinking with respect to Toussaint Louverture has been renewed in recent years with what the late Chris Bayly described in 2010 as 'the "conservative turn" in the global history of the revolutionary age'.[24] This new revisionist scholarship with respect to the Haitian Revolution is perhaps most clearly represented in the work of Philippe Girard, whose *Toussaint Louverture: A Revolutionary Life* (2016) was marketed as 'the definitive biography of one of the most influential men of the modern era'.[25] Girard's biography, it must be said at the outset, is indeed a finely written and evocative work, particularly impressive in the depth of the archival research undertaken in the detailed reconstruction of Louverture's early life, and its contribution deserves to be acknowledged by every scholar and student of the Haitian Revolution. Yet politically, the conservatism shaping Girard's underlying argument about Louverture is unmistakeable. In his view, it is no longer apparently 'accurate' to maintain that 'Louverture was the idealistic herald of slave emancipation, the forefather of an independent Haiti, and a black nationalist'. Rather, for Girard, above all, he was a pragmatist . . . if we examine Louverture solely through the prism of our current preoccupations with race, slavery, and imperialism, we risk missing the issues that mattered to *him*, starting with his personal ambition . . . his craving for social status was a constant. Educating himself, seeing to his children's future, making money, gaining and retaining power, and achieving recognition as a great man: he never wavered from the pursuit of these ends. He was a social climber and a self-made man . . . .[26]

If Pluchon domesticated Louverture's revolutionary 'black Jacobinism' by portraying him instead as essentially a figure of the *ancien régime* and aspiring member of the master planter class, Girard's Louverture appears more like a would-be member of the bourgeois capitalist class with an individualistic atavistic mentality; indeed, at one point Girard suggests that his portrayal of Louverture as, 'in many ways, a citizen of the modern, capitalist world' in fact 'humanizes a figure who can seem unapproachable otherwise'.[27] While Louverture was, of course, 'in many ways, a citizen of the modern, capitalist world' – given slave ships, sugar plantations and so on were some of the most advanced and modern forms of capitalist production of their day – in fact simply to regard him above all as a personally ambitious aspiring bourgeois does not 'humanise' him – it *reduces* him to merely one fragment of his life and personality.[28]

Indeed, leaving aside Girard's deeply problematic assumption that Louverture's commitment to 'educating himself' is a signifier of an inherent 'craving for social status' (rather than something that arguably places him as part of a long-standing strong autodidactic tradition within radical and revolutionary political thought),[29] it might be remembered that Louverture was not – and never claimed to be – a revolutionary until the revolution erupted in the last dozen years of his life. As a black person living in a non-revolutionary situation in a barbaric slave society, where black people could be killed on a whim by white people as a matter of course, with little (if any) chance of any legal or other repercussions, sheer survival and *existence* represented in itself a form of *resistance*.

Moreover, once the revolution began in 1791, it is surely a little odd to maintain that Louverture was 'above all' a 'pragmatist' concerned with 'personal ambition', 'social status' and 'making money'. Such a person, it might be suggested, would be an unlikely person repeatedly to risk life and limb by putting themselves on the frontline of a black slave army fighting under the banner of 'Liberty or death' – and indeed, would be the least likely person to be able to inspire others to follow him into battle under such a slogan. If Louverture had wanted money and status above all, there were surely safer ways to try and secure them, even once the revolt had begun. Indeed, rather than seeing Louverture essentially as a 'self-made man', we would re-iterate the point made by C.L.R. James, who stressed that on a fundamental level 'it was the revolution that made Toussaint'.[30]

As well as implicitly seeking to downplay Louverture's commitment to revolutionary ideas, Girard also attempts to domesticate Louverture's blackness, suggesting that Louverture 'was no black nationalist' but instead 'an aspiring Frenchman', and as governor of colonial Saint-Domingue 'would do his best to imitate' the 'mannerisms' of the white former master planter class and 'become a "big white" in his turn'.[31] As Girard puts it at one point, if 'the most enthusiastic white converts to the Revolution were known as "white blacks"; in many ways he was a "black white" who had made the economic world view of his former masters his own'.[32] This seems to us to be, at best, very *one-sided*, given Louverture was the central figure in the leadership of the Haitian Revolution, a foundational struggle for self-determination which was – among other things – inherently also a struggle for 'Black Power' in an Atlantic world dominated by slavery and a system of white supremacy under the flags of competing European colonial powers. Even though Louverture himself never pushed for outright independence for Saint-Domingue, he represented a major challenge to French colonial domination nonetheless. As for his 'imitating' the 'mannerisms' of 'big whites', C.L.R. James notes that in 1798, at a time when 'the whites of Port-au-Prince were bowing and scraping before him, an incident took place which lets us see what Toussaint thought of the whites as whites'.

A white colonist wanted a post as storekeeper and asked Toussaint for it. Toussaint said no. The colonist's wife tried many times to approach Toussaint, but was unsuccessful. Some time after she gave birth to a son and asked Toussaint to be the godfather. Toussaint, usually so suave and conciliatory, for some reason or other, decided to let this woman know his mind.

'Why, Madame, do you wish me to be godfather of your son – your approach to me has no other aim than to get me to give a post to your husband, for the feelings of your heart are contrary to the request that you make of me.'

'How can you think so, General? No, my husband loves you, all the whites are attached to you.'

'Madame, I know the whites. If I had their skin – yes, but I am black and I know their aversion to us . . . After my death, who knows if my brothers will not be driven back into slavery and will yet perish under the whip of the whites . . . the French Revolution has enlightened Europeans, we are loved and wept over by them, but the white colonists are enemies of the blacks . . . You wish your husband to get a post. Well, I give him the employment he demands. Let him be honest and let him remember that I cannot see everything, but that nothing escapes God. I cannot accept your offer to be godfather to your son. You may have to bear the reproaches of the colonists and perhaps one day that of your son.'[33]

Whilst acknowledging biographical and historical uncertainties, the aim of our work is then to challenge versions of Louverture that aim to accommodate him to the norms and values of *our* age of late capitalism, and to reassert the incendiary political implication of *his* life, actions and revolutionary political thought. In this sense, we are openly situating ourselves in the tradition of radical historical scholarship of the Haitian Revolution best exemplified by C.L.R. James, and our subtitle, referring to Toussaint as a 'black Jacobin', is in part to pay explicit homage to James's masterwork. In the face of a growing conservative revisionist scholarship on Louverture's life, which would like to bury what it dismisses as the 'ethical' or 'idealist' interpretation, it remains important to defend the intellectual and theoretical ground which James and *The Black Jacobins* – and those scholars who have followed in James's footsteps, such as Robin Blackburn, Carolyn Fick and Laurent Dubois – have battled so hard to win in the field of Haitian Revolutionary studies.

A Black Jacobin in the Age of Revolutions

The second part of our subtitle returns to the importance of situating Louverture in his concrete historical context, stressing the fact that he lived in 'an age of revolutions'. That great 'citizen of the world' Thomas Paine probably deserves credit for coining the phrase, when he wrote in *The Rights of Man*, published in 1791, '[i]t is an age of Revolutions, in which every thing may be looked for'.[34] The Haitian Revolution, which erupted the same year as *The Rights of Man* was published, triumphantly vindicated Paine's prognosis. It not only followed the other great 'Atlantic revolutions' of the period, such as the American War of Independence and the French Revolution, but by abolishing slavery for good in what was then the prized French sugar plantation colony of Saint-Domingue, went far further than the other two revolutions in its commitment to the principle of universal emancipation and human rights for all. Yet the historians most famously associated with early work on 'the age of revolutions' – such as R.R. Palmer, author of *The Age of the Democratic Revolution: A Political History of Europe and America, 1760–1800* (two volumes, 1959–64) and Jacques Godechot, author of *France and the Atlantic Revolution of the Eighteenth Century, 1770–1799* (1965) – like the vast majority of other Western scholars, manifestly failed to register the importance of the Haitian Revolution. In the context of the Cold War and NATO, Palmer explicitly stated that for him the 'age of revolutions' was about 'the Revolution of the Western world', a 'Revolution of Western Civilisation', and 'the Revolution of the non-Western' did not come until the twentieth century.[35] Even though Palmer had read *The Black Jacobins*, which in many ways deserves to be hailed as the genuine pioneering work on 'Atlantic history' and 'Atlantic Revolutions', he still, as Lynn Hunt notes, 'devoted only one page to the Haitian Revolution in the second volume of his work on the Atlantic revolutions. He had ten pages on the failed Polish revolution of 1794'.[36]

As well as drawing attention to the critical transnational dimensions of revolutionary thought and struggle that erupted during Louverture's lifetime, our subtitle is also designed to pay a certain mark of respect not only to Thomas Paine, but to the late great historian Eric Hobsbawm, author of works including *The Age of Revolution: Europe, 1789–1848* (1962). Though Hobsbawm focused primarily on the 'dual revolution – the rather more political French and the industrial (British) revolution' underway in Europe – he detested the idea of an emerging model of 'Atlantic history' that was designed to forgive and forget 'European expansion in and conquest of the rest of the world', and instead glorified 'Western Civilisation'. For Hobsbawm, 'the age of revolution' was part of a 'world revolution' which 'spread outward from the double crater of England and France' and included within it anti-colonialism and anti-imperialism, the beginnings of what he called 'the world-wide revolt against the west, which dominates the middle of the twentieth century'. Hobsbawm had not only read but more critically absorbed the essence of James's argument in *The Black Jacobins* about the importance of the Haitian Revolution. In *The Age of Revolution*, Hobsbawm accordingly registered that in 1794 the Jacobins 'abolished slavery in the French colonies, in order to encourage the Negroes of San Domingo to fight for the Republic against the English', something which had 'the most far-reaching results' including helping 'to create the first independent revolutionary leader of stature' in the Americas in the figure of Toussaint Louverture.[37]

Before the Jacobin leader Maximilien Robespierre became a revolutionary, Richard Cobb noted that he 'marinated in over ten years of genteel poverty and social resentment in a small provincial town'.[38] Our work begins by seeking to explore how Toussaint himself 'marinated' over a much longer period in the very different environment of the barbaric and brutal sugar plantation colony of Saint-Domingue – a highly prosperous French colony that, in 1789, began to come apart at its seams under the impact of the outbreak of revolution in France itself. Our understanding of Toussaint's 'marination' has been greatly assisted by the archival work of a number of historians, conducted most notably by Haitian pioneers such as Jean Fouchard, and extended more recently by David Geggus, Philippe Girard and others. As the subtitle of our work suggests, however, there is at the same time a critical need to understand details gleaned not only in the context of Saint-Domingue and the French empire of the *ancien régime*, but also in the frame of the political, philosophical and cultural histories of the Enlightenment and the wider Atlantic world, a world that was soon about to be thrown into turmoil. As the great Enlightenment *philosophe* Jean-Jacques Rousseau prophetically noted amidst the Seven Years War (1756–63) in *Émile* (1762), 'we are approaching the state of crisis and the century of revolutions'.[39]

1

Toussaint Unchained,
c. 1743–91

I was born a slave, but nature gave me the soul of a free man.[1]

The man who would later be known by the name Toussaint Louverture was born into slavery in the early 1740s. The exact date of his birth is likely to remain unknown, and many accounts of his early years contain contradictory or unverifiable information that suggests they are derived largely from legend. Before moving to address these details, it is helpful to understand the environment into which he was born and in which the foundations for his revolutionary life were laid. Saint-Domingue, the colony of Louverture's birth, had – with the landing of Columbus on Hispaniola in 1492 – been the location of what is generally regarded as one of the first contacts between Europeans and indigenous peoples of the Americas. The Spanish were the first to attempt to settle the island, which is now still shared by Haiti and the Dominican Republic. Columbus returned to Spain to report his 'discovery' to the King, but the crew of one of his ships, the wrecked *Santa Maria*, built the first European settlement at Navidad, triggering revolts by the indigenous population, the leaders of whom were summarily executed. Most notable among these first Haitians to resist foreign incursion and attempts at colonisation was Anacaona, tricked and captured by the Spanish in ways that many see as paralleling the treatment of Toussaint Louverture three centuries later. The Western diseases that accompanied the Spanish, as well as their brutal treatment and overwork of the local population, also led to a rapid decline in numbers of the Taino Indians.

By the later sixteenth century, although the Spanish had established the first court of their crown in the Americas at Santo Domingo in 1526, their colonial ambitions began to focus elsewhere, particularly on mainland North and South America, and the colony fell into decline. In the early 1600s, however, in the context of growing European rivalry around New World Territories, Hispaniola again become the subject of attention. Initially it was French sailors, merchants and pirates – known as *boucaniers* as a result of the *boucans*, or open fires, on which they cooked the wild cattle and pigs on which they relied for food – who settled on Tortuga, an island north of present-day Port-de-Paix, and used this as the base for their operations in the region. In 1635, elsewhere in the Caribbean, the French claimed for their empire Martinique and Guadeloupe, as well as what is today French Guiana; two decades later, they had also taken control of Tortuga in addition to the settlements in the north of the mainland of Hispaniola. In a context of imperial rivalry with Spain, the French appointed a governor to Saint-Domingue in 1665, consolidating the division of the island that, despite several periods of unification (not least under Toussaint Louverture), persists today.

In 1697, with the Treaty of Ryswick, Spain formally handed control of western Hispaniola to France, and this colony – now renamed Saint-Domingue – was set to become a key asset in the French Atlantic and a major contributor to France's national economy. The reliance for this wealth creation on brutally enslaved labour was disguised in the colony's popular designation as the 'pearl of the Antilles', a misleading label that still retains currency today.[2] The cultivation of sugar, reliant on the use of enslaved African labour, was already well established in the Caribbean by this time and, from the early eighteenth century, Saint-Domingue was increasingly recognised for its potential to cater for growing demand for the product in Europe. To establish their authority in this new context, the French had already encouraged planters to settle, and they developed a brutal and dehumanising trade in enslaved Africans transported across the Atlantic to work on tobacco, indigo and sugar plantations, activities to which the cultivation of coffee was added in the eighteenth century as a new cash crop that proved easier and cheaper to grow. By the time of the Revolution, there was also significant production of cotton adding to the wealth generated for plantation owners and their metropolitan investors.

Across the eighteenth century, numbers of settlers and of the enslaved population grew exponentially, rising from over 6,000 whites and some 35,000 enslaved people in 1715 to over 32,000 whites and almost 250,000 enslaved people in 1779 (with estimates suggesting that the numbers of the enslaved had nearly doubled during the next decade by the time of the outbreak of the Haitian Revolution).[3] The extensive colonisation and agricultural exploitation of Saint-Domingue led to divisions – administrative and otherwise – that would continue to impact on Haiti throughout the Revolution and into the independence period. Sugar plantations were situated in the northern part of the island, where the land was flat and well-irrigated; the southern peninsula was the last part of the island to attract settlers, and the less agriculturally fertile southern part of the colony was associated more generally with the sphere of influence of the administrative centre of Port-au-Prince. Although the early agriculture in the French Caribbean colonies depended on the labour of white indentured workers in addition to that of enslaved Africans, the figures above reveal a progressive reliance on the Atlantic slave trade and the transformation of Saint-Domingue into a plantation economy – or more accurately a 'slave society' in which enslavement impacted on every aspect of life. During Toussaint's lifetime, the future leader of the revolution would, therefore, have seen major transformations in the society and economy in which he lived, especially following the end of the Seven Years' War in 1763, when Europeans – returned to a period of relative peace – sought ever increasing quantities of sugar and coffee, the exotic commodities for which they had rapidly developed a taste. As we have noted, during the three decades before the outbreak of the Haitian Revolution, the population of Saint-Domingue nearly doubled, with the importation of enslaved Africans reaching almost 30,000 a year by the late 1780s. Cap Français, the colonial capital, was a busy port, constructed along the lines of a major cosmopolitan European city, but these trappings of civilisation did little to obscure the brutality of a plantation system as well as the significant social and ethnic divisions that defined the colony.

Contesting the denial of freedom was engrained in the histories of slavery: the enslaved Africans in Saint-Domingue were subject to brutal exploitation, but managed nevertheless to develop their own social and religious practices – not least Vodou, a combination of aspects of Christianity with elements of African religions that became particularly apparent in the eighteenth century. *The Black Jacobins* opens with C.L.R. James's assertion that, despite the ways in which slavery dehumanised those whose liberty it removed, the enslaved remained 'quite invincibly human beings',[4] with significant evidence of that humanity reflected in the ubiquity of individual acts of resistance, in practices such as induced abortion, infanticide and poisoning. Many of the enslaved also escaped and sought to establish maroon communities in less accessible locations (most notably the *mornes*, or mountains, from which their name was derived). Although there were no major slave rebellions in Saint-Domingue before 1791, a series of unexplained deaths and poisonings in 1757–58 were blamed on Mackandal, a Haitian maroon leader who, like Toussaint Louverture, was known for his knowledge of plants and herbs. Captured, tortured and burnt at the stake in Cap Français, Mackandal is still celebrated in Haitian collective memory, and encapsulates the simmering spirit of resistance that would culminate in the outbreak of the Revolution itself and that formed part of the environment into which Toussaint Louverture was born.

'Worked like animals,' notes C.L.R. James, 'the slaves were housed like animals [. . .] Defenceless against their masters, they struggled with overwork and its usual complement – underfeeding.'[5] Living and working conditions were atrocious, and life expectancy – especially for the enslaved who worked on plantations and not in domestic contexts – was startlingly low: up to one in three of those who had been forced into slavery and brought to the Caribbean from Africa died within a year of their arrival. In 1685, the French had introduced the *Code Noir* to regulate (in theory at least) these conditions, stipulating amounts of food to be provided (significantly below what would be considered healthy), but also permitting plantation owners to use whipping and other forms of violence and terror to discipline those they enslaved. The code also stated that owners had the right to free their slaves, and at the same time allowed the enslaved, provided their owners approved, to purchase their own freedom. This meant that, by the time of the outbreak of the Revolution in 1791, there was a significant free black population in Saint-Domingue, including by that time Louverture himself, a number of whom owned property (extending to slaves) in their own right. Other free people of colour, usually descended from white fathers and black mothers – sexual relationships which in large part were testament to the oppressive power relations of this slave society – formed part of the complex social mix of the colony. Responsible for running businesses and increasingly involved in the politics and economics of Saint-Domingue, the group known dismissively as 'mulattoes' attracted growing hostility from the white population, who established in the colony clearly regulated ethnic hierarchies and sought to police access to certain professions and positions of authority. Emboldened by news of the outbreak of the French Revolution in 1789 with its revolutionary slogan 'Liberty, Equality, Fraternity', the coloured population would, in the period leading up the outbreak of its Haitian equivalent, seek the same liberties and rights as the white population.

The whites of Saint-Domingue were themselves, however, far from homogenous, ranging from *petit blancs* (workers, sailors, vagrants) at the bottom of the social hierarchy, to the *grand blancs* (merchants, plantation owners) who earnt fortunes and increasingly resented what they saw as the meddling of the French metropolitan government in their lives. (1768 saw a rebellion of the colonists, who sought authority to control the free coloured population as their wealth and power grew, threatening the status quo of the colony's social and economic structures.) Also in this ethnic group were the plantation managers and overseers, hired to operate plantations in their owners' absence, and often directly responsible for physical brutality and financial exploitation.

The enslaved themselves were divided into two principal groups, *bossales* and *creoles*, the former recently transported from Africa to the Caribbean and forced to adapt to the conditions imposed upon them, the latter born in the colony itself to parents already living in slavery. Given the rapid expansion of numbers of the enslaved in Saint-Domingue in the years leading up to the outbreak of the Revolution, the percentage of *bossales* was high, and would have implications for the conduct of warfare during the struggle for independence as well as for attitudes towards authority (most notably royalty as opposed to republican representatives).

Family Background and Boyhood

The man who would in later life be known as Toussaint Louverture himself belonged to the category of *creole*, as it was his father who had been enslaved in Africa and endured the violence and terror of the Middle Passage across the Atlantic Ocean in a slave ship to the New World of the Americas, and specifically to Saint-Domingue. As an enslaved child, Toussaint would have been known in his early life as Toussaint Bréda, named after the plantation on which he was born. The traces of the enslaved in archives tend to be minimal, and Toussaint is no exception. He was moreover sparing with detail about his early life once he became prominent in the public sphere: his memoir, produced towards the end of his life during his imprisonment at Joux in 1802–03, focuses almost exclusively on the war of independence and discloses very little about his formative years. Details of his origins have often tended to be derived from highly mythologised accounts of his life produced by his contemporaries, with these supplemented by other material such as his son Isaac Louverture's own memoirs published in 1825. For a long time, it was Isaac who provided the main source of what had become the accepted version of the revolutionary's parentage and birth, linking his father to the royal dynasty of the Allada from Benin. His account of his own father's origins is, however, to be read with extreme caution for it depends on an oral account transmitted across a period of almost a century, and one that most likely sought to explain Louverture's statesmanlike qualities by stressing as aristocratic an ancestry as possible. In *Citizen Toussaint*, a much later Left Book Club biography of Louverture, Ralph Korngold presents the father of his subject as Hippolyte, the 'second son of an African chieftain named Gaou-Ginou',[6] who was captured with his wife Affiba and two children, first sold at the slave market in Dahomey, and then sold to the Bréda plantation at Haut de Cap in Saint-Domingue. In his recent work, Philippe Girard has questioned this account of origins, and suggests that Toussaint was of aristocratic rather than royal ancestry, seeing the creation of this genealogy as an attempt to reduce the stigma associated with being captured and trafficked into slavery.[7]

Notwithstanding continued uncertainty over origins, what remains clear is that enslavement rapidly and inevitably ended any privilege Toussaint Louverture's father might have enjoyed in his country of birth: as was often the case, his family – enslaved and sold alongside him – was split up on arrival in the Caribbean. It seems likely that Hippolyte's first wife and children were bought by a colonist and taken to a plantation in the south of Saint-Domingue. Hippolyte himself, taken to the Bréda plantation, remarried an enslaved woman called Pauline. In discussing Louverture's origins, Korngold's account sows some seeds of doubt, caused by allusions in the revolutionary leader's own memoir to his 105-year-old father, but subsequent research has suggested that these references seem to relate instead to his godfather, Pierre Baptiste. As Girard comments: 'retracing the childhood of a slave is an arduous task',[8] not only because of the lack of archival traces, but also because such traces that exist tend to dehumanise the enslaved and deny their individuality. We have also suggested, in part on the evidence of the memoir that Toussaint would subsequently compose towards the end of his life, that the future revolutionary leader appears to have been keen to maintain a degree of obscurity around his origins. The records of the Bréda plantation (owned at that time by the Comte de Noé, and managed on his behalf by Bayon de Libertat) for the period before 1785 have in any case been lost, but most biographies claim that the first of Hippolyte and Pauline's five children was born there around 1743 (although alternative dates proposed vary from the late 1730s to 1756). The actual date of Toussaint's birth remains uncertain, but from his name it is often assumed he was born on All Saints' Day.

As with the detail of his birth, about Louverture's youth we know very little. Legend claims that Toussaint was a sickly child, nicknamed 'Fatras-Bâton' (literally 'little stick'), who had defied his parents' doubts about his ability to survive by subjecting himself from an early age to a physical regime that meant he could swim, jump and ride horses in a way that surpassed the abilities of his peers. We have no reason to doubt that Toussaint's childhood differed in any way from others born into slavery in Saint-Domingue. His mother would almost certainly have returned to labour on the Bréda plantation shortly after her pregnancy, but Toussaint would have been introduced through storytelling to tales of the culture, history and traditions of his father's home. Accounts of Toussaint's early life also often insist on his more formal education, and suggest evidence of his advanced literacy to underline his exceptional character and to explain how he rose to lead the revolution. Opinions are divided as to his written skills, but it is clear that as a revolutionary leader he relied heavily on secretaries for drafting documents and correspondence, and texts we have in French produced in his hand are described as 'strictly phonetic'.[9]

Philippe Girard has indicated that although Toussaint's mother tongue would have been Fon, the language of his parents spoken in Benin, he would have acquired Kreyòl in his childhood and subsequently, as a means of social advancement, sought to master standard French.[10] Dominicans and Jesuits were present in Saint-Domingue during the eighteenth century, seeking to convert the enslaved population and steer them away from syncretic religious practices associated with Vodou. Girard notes that the enslaved on the Bréda plantation were joined in a daily act of prayer,[11] and it seems likely that Toussaint received instruction from Jesuits before their expulsion from Saint-Domingue in the 1760s as well as later from his godfather, Pierre Baptiste. Operating trilingually in his adult life, he almost certainly deployed these languages strategically, according to the interlocutors with whom he was faced. The acquisition of French and the possibility that Toussaint also read Latin are aspects central to C.L.R. James's understanding of his character. Iconic scenes of reading also feature in illustrations of his childhood and youth, most notably in Jacob Lawrence's 41-panel sequence of his life, produced in the context of the Harlem Renaissance. *The Black Jacobins* describes the young Toussaint reading a series of key texts that served as preparation for his future role: Caesar's commentaries, a source of understanding of politics and the art of war; Raynal's *Histoire des deux Indes* ('History of the two Indies'), a popular multi-authored and encyclopedic account of trade between Europe and the Far East, first published in 1780, that catered for a growing public appetite in the

Enlightenment for knowledge of the wider world. Raynal's text, if he indeed read it, would have provided Toussaint with information about Saint-Domingue itself, as well as about economic, political and commercial aspects of all the major Western empires.

The *Histoire des deux Indes* also contained a key passage, drawn from Louis-Sébastien Mercier's futuristic novel from 1771, *L'An deux mille quatre cent quarante* ('The Year 2440'), in which the emergence of a great leader of the enslaved against the forces of oppression is foretold:

> Where is he, this great man that Nature owes to its vexed, oppressed, tormented children? Where is he? He will appear [. . .] He will show himself and will raise the sacred banner of liberty. This venerable leader will gather around him his comrades in misfortune. More impetuous than torrents, they will leave everywhere ineffacable traces of their just anger.[12]

This passage is often cited as evidence of Toussaint's predestination for revolutionary leadership, and C.L.R. James describes in him a singularity and distinctiveness that suggests he enjoyed great respect amongst the enslaved of Saint-Domingue long before the struggle for emancipation became a reality:

> His comparative learning, his success in life, his character and personality gave him an immense prestige among all the Negroes who knew him, and he was a man of some consequence among the slaves long before the revolution. Knowing his superiority he never had the slightest doubt that his destiny was to be their leader, nor would those with whom he came in contact take long to recognise it.[13]

Toussaint's exceptionalism, seen as part of his constitution as a revolutionary leader, appears to have been embedded in the experience of his early years.

It is significant that Toussaint spent the period of his life when he was enslaved not working directly on the plantation, but in a series of roles in which he dealt with his owner's livestock and horses, exploiting his early equestrian skills and supplementing these with traditional veterinary knowledge. C.L.R. James, whose account of the future revolutionary leader before 1791 is remarkably brief, claims he was a steward, a function that gave him 'experience in administration, authority, and intercourse with those who ran the plantation'.[14] Madison Smartt Bell presents him also as a 'trusted retainer', acting as coachman for Bayon de Libertat – a role that would have given him considerable autonomy, and allowed him to travel around the colony relatively unimpeded.[15] Although it is likely, as a result of his role, that Toussaint never suffered the cruel and extreme punishments that C.L.R. James outlines in detail in the early sections of *The Black Jacobins*, he would nevertheless have existed in an environment of everyday, almost casual violence exacted by the white population on the enslaved. The average life expectancy on the Bréda plantations was a mere 37 years.[16]

Toussaint lived in a society where as a black person, even if nominally 'free', the most minor slight to a white – of whatever status – could mean the end of his life, and racist attacks and murders were a fact of life. Girard relates one incident relating to Toussaint that happened while walking back from the Mass one day with his prayer book:

> According to the story, which he shared ten years later, 'a white man broke my head with a wooden stick while telling me 'do you not know that a negro should not read?' Louverture prudently begged for forgiveness and slipped away, a decision that likely saved his life. But he kept his blood-soaked vest as a reminder and neither forgot nor forgave. Running into the same man years later, after the outbreak of the slave revolt, he killed him on the spot.[17]

The extent to which Toussaint's life enslaved on the Bréda plantation served as an apprenticeship in revolution is difficult to ascertain, not least because it is also possible that he also spent time as a *commandeur*, one of the enslaved who was tasked with organising work gangs and meting out punishment. What is likely is that Toussaint managed to play a double game, engaging with the institutions, practices and expectations of the French colonisers whilst maintaining a simmering resentment towards the oppressive system in which he was enslaved. Elements of Toussaint's early life lend themselves to a more conservative interpretation: he appears to have engaged fully, for instance, with Catholicism, marrying an enslaved woman Cécile in a formal ceremony when he was aged about 18 and then later Suzanne, who would remain his wife throughout the period of the Revolution. As Girard notes, although Saint-Domingue was for the enslaved a challenging place to raise a family, not least because of the sexual predation of the masters and the desire of many of them to deny the right of those they considered their property to exist in family units, Toussaint managed to maintain, through his two marriages, an extensive network of relatives on whose loyalty he could rely:

> He had biological children, illegitimate children, a stepson, an adopted daughter, a stepmother, two biological parents, and two surrogate parents, along with a bewildering collection of nephews, siblings, goddaughters, and in-laws. This sprawling family network allowed him to cope with slavery; much later it would form the backbone of his revolutionary regime.[18]

Imprisoned at the end of his life, Louverture would tell Napoleon's interrogator Caffarelli that he had fathered 16 children, eleven of whom had predeceased him.[19] The combination of a wider frame of relations and acquaintances on whom he could depend, of an education, of an insider knowledge regarding the practices and institutions of the plantation economy, and of a reputation for trustworthiness in the eyes of the French (not least among the officials on the Bréda plantation) would subsequently serve as key aspects of Toussaint's rise to revolutionary power.

Toussaint as a Slave Owner

One aspect of his higher social standing was, however, for a long time ignored, not least because it seems that this is something Louverture himself actively and almost consistently suppressed following his rise to public prominence in the 1790s. It was only in the 1970s that historians discovered evidence that, by the time of the outbreak of the Revolution, Toussaint Louverture was not only a freeman but had also been a slave owner in his own right.[20] The source of this information was a baptismal record from April 1776 of a girl called Marie-Josèphe. Her godfather, who had been unable to attend the ceremony, was Toussaint himself, an annotation next to whose name in the archive reveals that by that time he was already a 'nègre libre', or free black.[21] As Philippe Girard has recently argued, the manumission of enslaved males was relatively rare, and it is likely that Toussaint was freed by Bayon de Libertat in the early 1770s, following a period he spent as a runaway at the beginning of that decade.[22] The motivations of the overseer on the Bréda plantation are likely to remain obscure, but the common explanation is that Bayon de Libertat, having recognised Toussaint's potential, sought to win his loyalty and deploy his talents to his advantage. Manumission brought with it, however, no automatic economic advantage, but by 1776 Toussaint had gathered the resource to become a slave owner – of a West African named Jean-Baptiste – in his own right, and by the end of the decade also possessed a modest plot of land.

Revelation of Toussaint's status as a free black citizen of Saint-Domingue may appear to dent his revolutionary pedigree; it explains, however, the ways in which over a period of almost two decades the future revolutionary leader enjoyed a relative freedom to circulate in the colony, enhancing his knowledge of the geography of this part of the island, extending his network of contacts and consolidating his own power base. The article revealing Toussaint's manumission also provided evidence that in 1779 he took out a lease from his son-in-law on a coffee estate worked by 13 slaves. The venture was eventually unsuccessful and lasted no more than two years, but it allowed the future revolutionary leader to understand in detail the workings of the colony, and in particular the galvanisation by the planter class of the racial hierarchies on which it was founded. It is also likely that Toussaint manumitted several of the enslaved he purchased, supporting the claim by Girard and Donnadieu that his brief period as a slave owner was an example of 'altruism more than exploitation'.[23] His response to the failure of this enterprise was to return to the Bréda plantation, where he appears to have resumed his previous occupations, and it was around this time that his first marriage to Cécile also seems to have faltered.

For the decade before the outbreak of the Revolution, therefore, Toussaint worked as a salaried coachman for Bayon de Libertat, still overseer of the plantation, who had manumitted him several years earlier. He was a trusted figure, with the plantation accountant in 1785 describing him as a 'sweet' and 'intelligent subject, knowing how to care for injured animals'.[24] It was during this time that he married his second wife Suzanne Simon-Baptiste, a laundress enslaved on the Bréda plantation, and a key figure in his later life: Toussaint adopted Suzanne's son Placide, the offspring of mixed ethnicity of a previous relationship, and together they had two sons, Isaac (born 1784, and author of the memoir alluded to above) and Saint-John (born in the year of the outbreak of the Revolution, 1791). It was Suzanne who would take close control of her husband's financial affairs during the Revolution, and who would accompany him into enforced exile in France as the War of Independence approached its conclusion.

Saint-Domingue Enters a Revolutionary Situation

Lenin famously noted that there were three conditions for a revolutionary situation. The first, he stated, was that the ruling classes were no longer able to carry on ruling in the old way, that 'the upper classes were sufficiently at loggerheads with each other and had significantly weakened themselves in a struggle which is beyond their strength'.[25] As we have seen, there were all sorts of divisions among the white colonial elite, most obviously between the rich and propertied on the one hand (those the enslaved called *grand blancs* ['big whites'] or *Blancs blancs* ['White whites']) – and the poor *petit blancs* ['little whites'] on the other.[26] There were also inherent tensions amongst the richest and most powerful figures on Saint-Domingue: between on the one hand the master planter class, who were resentful of any attempts to compromise their autonomy and dreamt of ultimate national independence from France and the freedom to trade on the open market with other countries like Britain for the best price, and so better enrich themselves, and on the other the colonial bureaucratic elite, direct representatives of the French authorities and Bourbon monarchy, who governed in the interests of the metropole. There was resentment throughout the 1780s at French attempts to intervene in the affairs of Saint-Domingue, particularly concerning amelioration of the conditions of the enslaved (or at least proper implementation of legislation designed to protect them), and this would soon engender a paradoxical situation that Girard succinctly outlines: 'advocates of independence were reactionaries, while rebel slaves were staunch royalists'.[27]

But all these internal and external contradictions did not fully manifest themselves until 1789, when the Great French Revolution exploded in Paris, symbolised by the storming of the Bastille. The white planters of Saint-Domingue, like those in other French colonies, now took the opportunity to join war on the representatives of the absolute Bourbon monarchy, splitting white society between supporters of the revolution, 'the Patriots', and counter-revolutionary royalists. Soon white Saint-Domingue, like France itself, was in a state of civil war. The local planter class were perhaps inspired by the American Revolution, which had succeeded in ending the colonial domination of Britain while – crucially for the owners of the plantations – leaving intact the profitable institution of slavery. Yet as the local planter class were soon to find out, trying to make an elite 'revolution from above' in the name of 'liberty' while presiding over the most obscene form of tyranny imaginable was to prove easier said than done.

The second condition Lenin suggested for a revolutionary situation was that 'all the vacillating, wavering, unstable, intermediate elements' of society 'had sufficiently exposed themselves in the eyes of the people' and bankrupted themselves politically.[28] In Saint-Domingue, there existed a fair number of wavering, intermediate elements in society between the white planter class and the masses of black slaves, yet most significant here was the 28,000-strong free coloured population, the mixed heritage so-called 'mulattoes'.[29] Many free people of colour were rich and powerful planters who owned slaves themselves, while others lived a poorer existence and probably identified somewhat more with the plight of the enslaved black community. Yet while economically the free people of colour were quite powerful, and numerically they matched the whites, politically and legally they were excluded and discriminated against on the grounds of their ethnicity. The free people of colour – some 941 of whom, including leading figures like André Rigaud, had fought as light infantrymen as part of the *Chasseurs volontaires* for the French during the American War of Independence – saw in the French Revolution of 1789 a chance to stake their claim as 'men' and so challenge the rule of white supremacy on the island and at last get political equality.[30] Their arguments increasingly carried some weight in revolutionary France itself, where a transformation of mass consciousness was now underway, against not only the aristocracy of birth but increasingly also against racism, the 'aristocracy of the skin'.

However, in Saint-Domingue, the powerful white elite sought – through local legislation and political action – to anticipate any impact on their own society, and were particularly hostile towards the free coloured population. The treatment of Vincent Ogé, a free coloured planter who spent time in Paris following the Revolution seeking to extend suffrage to his ethnic group, is exemplary in this regard. Returning to Saint-Domingue, he escaped arrest and threatened to deploy force to extract the right to vote. In a letter to the governor of the colony, de Peinier, he wrote: 'we will not remain under the yoke as we have for two centuries. The iron rod that has beaten us down is broken. [. . .] Be prudent, therefore, and avoid a crisis that you would not be able to subdue.'[31]

Ogé's planned insurrection in the North in late 1790 was short-lived and violently repressed. Once captured, he (and his fellow co-conspirator Jean-Baptiste Chavannes) were executed in a barbaric fashion, broken on a wheel in a manner designed to elicit fear from anyone considering a similar challenge to the status quo. Nineteen others were also hanged.[32] Commentators on Ogé's tactics have criticised his failure to harness the rights of the free coloured population to the desire of the enslaved for their own liberation. Had he yoked the simmering desire for revolt amongst the enslaved black masses to his own political aspirations, the outcome might have been radically different. Ogé's rebellion served nevertheless as a key stage in the emerging logic of the Haitian Revolution itself. It is likely that Toussaint knew Ogé, and possible he was a witness to his execution.[33]

In response to the act of defiance on the part of the white planters in Saint-Domingue, the National Assembly passed a law in May 1791 granting voting rights to any coloured inhabitant of the colony whose two parents were also free. The intervention was a modest one, but reasserted the principle that Paris could continue to legislate on issues relating to ethnicity in Saint-Domingue. The reaction of the *grand blancs* in the colony, clearly alarmed that their power base could be further eroded and that – as would indeed be the case only three years later – the general emancipation of the black population might follow, was one of outrage. In the south of Saint-Domingue, the free coloured population organised itself militarily, and fought the local whites. But in these early battles, the free people of colour, while championing the ideals of liberty and equality, themselves maintained their deadly silence on the question of slavery. Yet without the enslaved, militarily they could not really hope to defeat the whites, while politically their dream of simply replacing the whites as the ruling planter class of Saint-Domingue was a bankrupt one, and ultimately left them as a group helpless and exposed.

The third and final condition for a revolutionary situation, Lenin suggested, was that the ruled themselves should no longer be prepared to tolerate being ruled in the old way, that 'a mass sentiment among the exploited and oppressed masses in favour of supporting the most determined, supremely bold, revolutionary action has arisen and begun vigorously to grow'.[34] And here we come to the black enslaved masses themselves, whose miserable existence, being forcibly worked to an early death on the sugar plantations, meant they were generally somewhat predisposed to meeting this condition of demanding revolutionary emancipation from their condition at all times and places across the Americas. Indeed, the French colony of Saint-Domingue had always looked to far-sighted observers as though it was a sleeping volcano that could erupt into social revolution at any moment. The master planter class, the comte de Mirabeau noted in 1789, were 'sleeping at the foot of Vesuvius'. It was a matter not simply of the exceptional brutality and relentless injustices the planters meted out against their slaves that cried out at some point to be avenged, but of the balance of forces. By the time of the outbreak of the French Revolution in 1789, the over 30,000 whites lived amidst some 500,000 enslaved blacks.[35] When Vincent Ogé, the leader of the doomed uprising in 1790 of the free people of colour, was being tortured to death by his white captors, apparently 'he took black powder or seedgrains in the hollow of his hand . . . sprinkled a film of white ones on the top, and said to his Judges, "Behold they are white;" then *shook* his hand and said, "Where are the whites, *Où sont les blancs?*"'[36]

Yet again the French Revolution was to play an important role in creating for the first time among the enslaved a feeling that supremely bold, revolutionary action could now potentially win as a strategy. News of the revolution in France rapidly crossed the Atlantic, and as historians such as Carolyn Fick have demonstrated, this took little time to enter the informal communication circuits of the enslaved themselves.[37] Many worked in domestic service and listened to the tense debates among the master planter class of Saint-Domingue. Accordingly, as James noted, 'they had heard of the revolution and had construed it in their own image: the white slaves in France had risen, and killed their masters, and were now enjoying the fruits of the earth. It was gravely inaccurate in fact, but they had caught the spirit of the thing. Liberty. Equality. Fraternity.'[38] Of course the proclamation of these new ideals by the revolutionary government in France had not led to any immediate change in the lives of the enslaved across the French Empire whatsoever, and The Declaration of the Rights of Man and the Citizen in 1789 did not mention slavery, just as it did not mention women. Indeed, it stated that property rights were sacred, and the enslaved after all were property. But such revolutionary declarations had nonetheless thrown the minority free population of Saint-Domingue into turmoil and civil war in the name of liberty, and now at least a minority among the enslaved saw their opportunity to strike out on their own for freedom, and began to plan accordingly.

Toussaint had witnessed all these developments, and undoubtedly already understood them in their wider revolutionary frame. 'As soon as unrest began in Saint-Domingue, I saw that the whites could not last, because they were divided and heavily outnumbered', he later recalled.[39] By 1789, Toussaint – now around 45 years old – had reached an age by which many of the enslaved in Saint-Domingue were already dead. As C.L.R. James notes, in the light of his qualities, experience and standing, his role in the emerging events was unsurprising: 'From the moment he joined the revolution he was a leader, and moved without serious rivalry to the first rank.'[40] As will become clear in the next chapter, however, and as James's observation implies, his involvement in the revolution was not immediate – although as a figure enjoying relative mobility and access to a variety of social contexts, it is likely that he would have been more aware than most of the rapidly evolving circumstances on both sides of the Atlantic. If his family had originally come from an aristocratic layer of African society in what is now Benin, Toussaint would soon find himself at the very forefront of fighting 'the aristocracy of the skin'. When he felt the time was right and the circumstances were favourable, he would be prepared to grasp the nettle, and provide – in the spirit of Raynal's call for that 'venerable leader [who] will gather around him his comrades in misfortune' – the leadership that would transform the pent-up violence of revolt into the strategy and tactics required for revolution.

2

Making an Opening to Liberty: 1791–93

After a series of mass meetings held at night in the northern mountain forests in early 1791, and inspired by Vodou priests such as the maroon 'Zamba' Boukman Dutty, the enslaved agreed to rise on Wednesday 24 August 1791 and take the great Northern port Cap Français (also known as Le Cap) at a time when the Colonial Assembly of Saint-Domingue was due to meet – giving them the chance to take out the island's political elite in one fell swoop.[1] Although there are divided opinions over its historical veracity, the Bois Caïman ceremony – presided over by Boukman Dutty and the mambo (priestess) Cécile Fatiman – is often seen as the starting point of the rebellion, and retains a significant symbolic value in Haiti as a result.[2] In the event, things did not quite go to plan and the rising began sporadically and a little prematurely in places, giving the planters just enough time adequately to defend Cap Français itself. Nevertheless, as C.L.R. James vividly described, on the night of Sunday 21 August 1791, 'a tropical storm raged, with lightning and gusts of wind and heavy showers of rain' and many of the leaders of the slave revolt met at Bois Caïman for a ceremony involving 'the sucking of the blood of a stuck pig' and to make final oaths in preparation for war:

> Carrying torches to light their way, the leaders of the revolt met in an open space in the thick forests of the Morne Rouge, a mountain overlooking Le Cap . . . That very night they began. Each slave gang murdered its masters and burnt the plantation to the ground . . . in a few days one half of the famous North Plain was a flaming

ruin. From Le Cap the whole horizon was a wall of fire. From this wall continually rose thick black volumes of smoke, through which came tongues of flame leaping to the very sky. For nearly three days the people of Le Cap could barely distinguish day from night, while a rain of burning cane straw, driven before the wind like flakes of snow, flew over the city and the shipping in the harbour, threatening both with destruction.[3]

The great mass of the enslaved in the North – the richest and most agriculturally developed region of Saint-Domingue – had finally made their move as one, rising under the slogan which originated in the American Revolution, 'Liberty or Death'. As Laurent Dubois notes, 'early in the insurrection, one group of insurgents presented a clear set of demands. They approached a French officer and told him they would surrender if 'all the slaves should be made free'. But they were 'determined to die, arms in hand, rather than to submit without a promise of liberty'. One executed insurgent was found to have 'in one of his pockets pamphlets printed in France, filled with commonplaces about the Rights of Man and the Sacred Revolution'.[4] If the enslaved themselves had not risen up against slavery, in what constituted the largest slave revolt in modern history, then as Dubois notes, 'the French Revolution would have probably run its course, like the American Revolution, without destroying the massive violation of human rights at the heart of the nation's existence'.[5] But it was not enough in itself for the enslaved to have risen in August 1791: any revolutionary movement that does not go forward does not stand still but goes backwards – and to go backwards would mean capture and, for the insurgents, certain death.

The black revolt in the North simply had to grow and spread, which it did, soon pulling behind it and into its ranks sections of more privileged groups such as free blacks and even at times – despite the earlier political dynamics described in the previous chapter – the free coloured population. From an initial rising of perhaps 1,000–2,000 insurgents on 23 August 1791, within a few days one report described them as 'now reckoned ten thousand strong, divided into three armies, of whom seven or eight hundred are on horseback'. By early September the size of the army had doubled to about 20,000, and by early October had doubled again to 40 or 50,000. By the end of November 1791, in the Northern Plain there may have been about 80,000 insurgents in open revolt (out of a total of about 170,000 enslaved people in that region of the colony), organised into different bands or camps akin to the different regiments of European armies.[6] One account from the fall of 1791 noted how in battle, the insurgents 'came forward dancing, shouting and singing, preceded by a great number of women and children, who served as ramparts'.[7]

Toussaint and the August 1791 Insurrection

That Toussaint Bréda would become one of the most important free black figures recruited into the leadership of this revolt is well known, but controversy still exists about the exact role he played during the August 1791 insurrection. Indeed, Madison Smartt Bell has even tried to breathe new life into what even he calls the 'royalist conspiracy theory' – explored by earlier biographers such as Ralph Korngold – by reasserting allegations levelled at Toussaint during his own lifetime, that he was the key organiser of the August 1791 insurrection, acting on behalf of counter-revolutionary forces, having been given the green light in desperation by the *grand blancs* of colonial Saint Domingue around Governor Blanchelande to do so. 'Their notion . . . was that a manufactured and secretly controlled uprising of the slaves on the Northern Plain could frighten the *petit blanc* faction', who had overthrown the old royalists and taken control of the Colonial Assembly at Cap Français, and restore the power of the *ancien régime* on the island.[8] For Bell, Toussaint's 'economic interests made him a natural partner of the *grand blancs*, as did a number of his personal ties and his involvement in Freemasonry'.[9] Despite noting that 'the tale . . . reduces the Haitian Revolution to a royalist conspiracy gone laughingly awry', Girard has attempted to reinforce Bell's argument nonetheless, suggesting that in order to convince the enslaved to rise up, Toussaint

employed the clever trick of implying that he was acting on behalf of the king of France . . . in return for rising up in his name, a grateful king would grant the rebels three days of rest a week . . . a century of progressive royal regulations had convinced the slaves that the mysterious French king who lived across the ocean was their most loyal defender.[10]

It is true that Toussaint had, among his many contacts, personal links with both the royalist faction and the early leaders of the insurgency, and seems to have possibly attended an important meeting of about 200 mostly privileged drivers or *commandeurs* in mid-August 1791 – preceding the Bois Caïman ceremony – on the Lenormand de Mézy estate, a large plantation at the foot of the Red Mountain. As David Geggus notes, 'on Sunday, August 14th a meeting of slave-drivers, coachmen, and other members of the "slave elite" from about 100 plantations took place in Plaine du Nord parish'. Geggus continues that news of Louis XVI's flight to Varennes had just reached the colony, and 'after discussions of political developments in France and the colony, they took the decision to rebel'.[11]

Toussaint at the very least would have certainly known about such meetings and the plans for such a revolt and indeed, had he wanted to, would have had no trouble attending this critical meeting. Yet there is no serious evidence that Toussaint played any such organising leadership role among the leaders of the insurgency at this stage, and the driving intellectual force at this point was undoubtedly – as has already been suggested – 'Zamba' Boukman Dutty, who had worked as a driver and coachman, and as Carolyn E. Fick notes was a Vodou priest whose 'authority was only enhanced by the overpowering impression projected by his gigantic size'.[12] Boukman Dutty's famous prayer delivered at this gathering, with its refrain of 'Couté la liberté li pale nan Coeur nous tous' – 'Listen to the voice of liberty which speaks in the hearts of all of us' – was unmistakably a call for a rising in the name of liberty and vengeance, not a rising at the behest of the French king:

The god who created the sun which gives us light, who rouses the waves and rules the storm, though hidden in the clouds, he watches us. He sees all that the white man does. The god of the white man inspires him with crime, but our god calls upon us to do good works. Our god who is good to us orders us to revenge our wrongs. He will direct our arms and aid us. Throw away the symbol of the god of the whites [the cross worn by Catholics around their necks] who has so often caused us to weep, and listen to the voice of liberty, which speaks in the hearts of us all.[13]

As the revolt began, and before it would be transformed into a revolution, Toussaint Bréda seems to have played no leading role, but remained on the Bréda plantation with the wife of his manager Bayon de Libertat, protecting the estate which remained more or less intact as the fires raged elsewhere around the Northern Plain. For Bell, 'a role as a deeply secret co-conspirator would help to explain how Toussaint was able to remain quietly and calmly unmolested at Bréda during the first several weeks of the insurrection, when all the surrounding plantations had been burned to ash', but the mere fact that Toussaint was a well-known and well-liked free black who in fact was *not* a 'natural partner' of the *grand blancs* in general might also be the clearest explanation of this.[14]

James suggests of Toussaint's behaviour here, in comparison with the most prominent insurgent leaders in August 1791 – such as Boukman Dutty, Jean-François Papillon, Georges Biassou and Jeannot Billet – that 'it seems certain that he had been in secret communication with the leaders, but like so many men of better education than the rank and file, he lacked their boldness at the moment of action and waited to see how things would go'.[15] This seems a more likely explanation than seeing Toussaint as Girard does, as 'the co-ordinator while others carried the rebel standard into battle'.[16] As Biassou himself put it, Toussaint 'proposed to me that we mobilize our comrades, but when the time came to get started, no one could convince him to act . . . Not daring to put himself at the head of our group, Toussaint begged me to make myself chief.'[17] While it is certainly not the case, as Bell asserts, that 'Toussaint had a large material investment in the colonial status quo' on Saint-Domingue, he did have a material investment of sorts, and appears at one time – as we have seen in the previous chapter – to have been a slave owner in his own right. Throwing himself into the revolt at this stage would certainly have meant cutting his personal ties with Bayon de Libertat who was busy trying to repress the black insurgency in the colonial militia.[18] As Girard notes, if the revolt failed, Bayon was 'the only one' who could vouch for Toussaint and 'prove that he was a freedman'.[19]

Equally though, the fact that Toussaint Bréda did not play any role in the revolt for the first month or so weakens the claim that the events were somehow an organised counter-revolutionary royalist conspiracy, with Toussaint playing a central role. Bell makes much of eyewitness accounts of the revolt, which assert that instead of rising in the name of 'liberty', apparently 'these rebels had nothing but white flags, white cockades; that their device was Vive Louis XVI, Roi de France et de Navarre; that their war cry was Men of the King; that they told themselves that they were under arms to re-establish the king on his throne, the nobility and the clergy in their privileges.'[20] Yet Bell himself gives one possible reason for the undoubted authority the insurgents gave to the king of France, which has nothing necessarily to do with a conscious counter-revolutionary 'royalist conspiracy' in play, when he argues that the insurgents – as we have suggested in the previous chapter – had an understanding 'that King Louis XVI wished them well and had created the *Code Noir* for their benefit, but that he himself was being held hostage by evil white men who surrounded him.'[21] Indeed, rumours along the lines that 'the king and the National Assembly in Paris had passed a decree abolishing use of the whip by masters and provided slaves three days a week instead of two' for themselves, and that troops from France were on their way to impose this new decree locally on Saint-Domingue had given confidence to those rebels gathered at the meeting on 14 August.[22] Perhaps for these reasons, as the insurgents stopped to regroup after a month or so of revolt, they formed themselves under the standard of monarchy, 'The King's Own', or the 'army of the king' to gain themselves a degree of legitimacy. Another important reason was the longstanding complex traditions of kingship in Africa, with both more absolutist and consensual forms of kingship experienced in the Kongo, for example. Dubois notes that 'the naming of 'kings' among the insurgents likely involved a transcultural dialogue between European and African visions of leadership and government'.[23]

Early Leadership in the Insurgency

'Zamba' Boukman Dutty, commanding wide respect and loyalty, was the main early inspirational leader of the insurgents, but in mid-November 1791, as Laurent Dubois notes, Dutty was 'gunned down during a battle' and then 'decapitated, his body burned by the French troops in view of the insurgent camps, and his head displayed on a stake in the main plaza of Le Cap'.[24] The main figures from the black insurgency who emerged now were Jean-François Papillon and Georges Biassou, both able leaders who could maintain control and discipline effectively in the aftermath of Dutty's death. Another leading figure, Jeannot Billet, was also establishing a reputation of sorts for his uncompromising nature and the brutal punishments he meted out to those he saw as enemies of the insurrection.

Jean-François Papillon, 'the supreme chief of the African army', was a former maroon who owed his command to his intellectual superiority, and wore a grey and yellow uniform decorated with a 'cross of Saint-Louis', an aristocratic military honour.[25] Jean-François took a somewhat elitist attitude towards the great mass of the black insurgents, assuring his French secretary Gros in October 1791 that 'in taking up arms, I have never pretended to fight for general liberty, which I know to be an illusion, as much due to France's need for her colonies as for the danger in granting to uncivilised hordes a right that would become infinitely dangerous to them, inevitably bringing about the destruction of the colony'.[26] Georges Biassou, Jean-François's second-in-command, who would steadily emerge as a rival, had been associated with a religious body called The Fathers of Charity,[27] yet was much more of a man of action and fighting. As the two wrote in late 1791, most of their followers were 'a multitude of *nègres* from the coast [Africa], most of whom can barely say two words of French but who in their country were accustomed to fighting wars'.[28] These African war veterans were experienced in skirmishing and forms of guerrilla warfare which were well suited to the mountainous and forested topography of colonial Saint-Domingue and meant they proved formidable adversaries for colonial forces from the very beginning.[29]

When Governor Blanchelande wrote to the insurgents, demanding they submit, they refused to do so. Their letter (dated 24 September 1791) is worth quoting at length as it reveals something of the complex ideological mix of ideas – in particular of kingship and the ideals of liberty – of the courageous fighters who had led the August 1791 insurrection:

Sir – We have never thought of failing in the duty and respect which we owe to the representative of the person of the King . . . but do you, who are a just man as well as a general, pay us a visit; behold this land which we have watered with our sweat – or rather, with our blood, – those edifices which we have raised and that in the hope of a just reward! Have we obtained it? . . . We are mistaken; those who, next to God, should have proved our fathers, have been tyrants, monsters unworthy of the fruits of our labours: and do you, brave general, desire that as sheep we should throw ourselves into the jaws of the wolf? No! it is too late.[30]

After stressing their refusal to submit to their monstrous tyrannical masters, the insurgent leaders – perhaps unsurprisingly given Biassou's religious faith – called on God 'who fights for the innocent' and who 'is our guide; he will never abandon us. Accordingly, this is our motto – Death or Victory!' The rebel leaders did propose a peaceful settlement to the colonial assembly, but this was an 'offer' which they knew the authorities were never going to accept, given that it demanded 'that all the whites . . . quit the Cape without a single exception'. In a final eloquent counter-blast, the black leaders noted the whites might have 'their gold and their jewels' but 'we seek only liberty, – dear and precious object!'

This, general, is our profession of faith; and this profession we will maintain to the last drop of our blood. We do not lack powder and cannons. Therefore, liberty or death! God grant that we may obtain freedom without the effusion of blood! Then all our desires will be accomplished; and believe it has cost our feelings very much to have taken this course. Victory or death for freedom![31]

By October 1791, Toussaint Bréda – having secured passages to relative safety elsewhere for his own family and Bayon and Madame de Libertat – had left his home at the Bréda plantation to join this band of insurgents, becoming an influential advisor to the second most important leader, the former *commandeur* Georges Biassou, now brigadier of the King's Army at Grand Boucan.[32] The two had probably known each other before the insurrection, and Biassou appointed Toussaint as his secretary and 'General Doctor' (on account of his knowledge of herbs). Toussaint's aptitude for leadership soon manifested itself beyond these responsibilities. On 15 October 1791, for example, we find Toussaint writing to Biassou asking for crowbars in order to dislodge rocks from the mountains of Haut de Cap to prevent the plantation owners' forces from approaching that way, and for barrows to transport wood to put up cabins at the tannery.[33]

Yet while the insurgents had shown they were more than capable of defending their existing positions, after four months the insurrection had found itself unable to spread to the West Province and break through the defensive line of white fortifications known as the Cordon of the West. As James notes, 'the former slaves could devastate the country around but that very devastation was making it impossible for them to exist. Famine began to kill them off'.[34] In desperation, on 12 December 1791, Jean-François Papillon and Georges Biassou decided to make an offer of peace to the three new French civil commissioners – Frédéric Ignace de Mirbeck, Philippe Roume de Saint Laurent, and Edmund de Saint-Léger – who had arrived in Cap Français from Paris.[35] They would end the revolt in return for an amnesty for 300 rebel leaders, the abolition of the whip and one extra day of freedom per week (i.e., three days rather than two) for the enslaved on the plantations. This was a very far cry from their original defiance in the face of Governor Blanchelande, and a betrayal of the rank and file of the insurgents by the black rebel leaders – Toussaint included – by any standard, and Jean-François and Biassou recognised that even if a deal could be agreed along these lines, not all the insurgents would acquiesce peacefully. 'Many *nègres* will hide in the woods; it will be necessary to pursue them diligently and to brave dangers and fatigue' to force them back to work, they told the French commissioners.[36]

Such a willingness to compromise with the old order was in keeping with Jean-François's earlier expressed elitist opposition to the idea of 'general liberty', and it is possible that one reason Jeannot Billet was arrested and executed by Jean-François in late 1791 was not simply for his notorious brutality and sadism towards white captives, but because Billet was a critical leading figure in his own right who stood in the way of Jean-François's willingness to strike a deal. As for Toussaint Bréda, his background, on the one hand, as a free black and his relationship with at least some of the colonial elite, on the other, perhaps help us understand why he was initially willing to act in late 1791 and early 1792 to try and help secure this negotiated settlement between the leaders of the black rebellion and the white planter class. Indeed, one hostile witness, General François Kerverseau, saw Toussaint as the critical figure among the insurgency in these negotiations:

He was the one who presided over the assembly at which Jean-François, Biassou, and others were chosen as leaders, because their size, strength, and other physical advantages seemed to suit them to a military command role. As for himself, puny and sickly, known to his comrades as *Skinny Stick*, he said he was only too honoured by the position of secretary to Biassou. It was from this obscure post to which he had relegated himself that, hidden behind a curtain, he served as a puppet master for the whole plot . . . He knew how to read and write, and he was the only one [among the leaders of the insurgency] who did.[37]

However, to the dismay of the civil commissioners, the rebel leaders' proposed offer was bluntly rebuffed by the white planters at the provincial assembly of the North, who, as James noted, simply 'could not understand that Biassou was no longer a slave but a leader of 40,000 men'.[38]

James goes on to argue that it was Toussaint's failed attempt to negotiate a secret deal that would see just 50 (rather than the previously agreed 300) rebel leaders free, in return for the peaceable return of the majority of the insurgents to slavery, that would be critical to his subsequent political evolution. Confronted with the utter intransigence of the planter class, James noted, 'then and only then did Toussaint come to an unalterable decision from which he never wavered and for which he died. Complete liberty for all, to be attained and held by their own strength.'[39] Despite not publicly agitating and taking a stand for 'general liberty' and the full abolition of slavery straightaway, Toussaint now nonetheless personally rejected the opportunity to take up the offer that was made by the colonial authorities for an amnesty for free people of colour after the National Assembly in France voted to abolish racial discrimination on 4 April 1792. Rather than defect to the white planters and play his part in the counter-insurgency operations then underway, Toussaint dropped his post of 'Physician to the Armies of the King' for the title of Brigadier-General and now emerged as a critically important military leader of the black rebel army (itself now loosely supported by the Spanish empire for its own ends), training up his own group of disciplined followers in the art of war – particularly guerrilla war.[40]

Toussaint had been busy, diligently learning the art of soldiering, and as Girard notes, 'a black veteran of the militia taught him basic drills, while a French prisoner he had spared gave him fencing lessons'.[41] As James comments in addition, 'it is characteristic of him that he began with a few hundred picked men, devoted to himself, who learnt the art of war with him from the beginning, as they fought side-by-side against the French troops and the colonists. In camp, he drilled and trained them assiduously'. From mid-1792, Toussaint – now with about 500 of the best revolutionary troops under his personal command – and the other rebel leaders were confident enough to make the argument for 'general liberty' based on the principle of natural human rights.[42]

In July 1792, the insurgent leaders Georges Biassou, Jean-François Papillon and Gabriel Aimé Belair wrote to the colonial assembly in Saint-Domingue and the national commissioner Roume.[43] This letter testifies to the return of a defiant spirit of boldness among the rebel leaders that had last been seen in their very first letter to Governor Blanchelande, and no doubt also to the pressure on them for 'general liberty' coming from the rank and file of the black insurgents. The letter dispensed with any declaration of loyalty to the king of France or, for that matter, reference to God, but instead was firmly couched and framed in the new language of the American and French Revolutions and the concept of natural rights and the Rights of Man flowing from Enlightenment *philosophes* like Jean-Jacques Rousseau. The letter reminded the colonial assembly that 'for a very long time . . . we have been victims of your greed and your avarice':

Under the blows of your barbarous whip we have accumulated for you the treasures you enjoy in this colony; the human race has suffered to see with what barbarity you have treated men like yourself – yes, men – over whom you have no other right except that you are stronger and more barbaric than we; you have engaged in [slave] traffic, you have sold men for horses, and even that is the least of your shortcomings in the eyes of humanity; our lives depend on your caprice, and when it's a question of amusing yourselves, the burden falls on men like us, who most often are guilty of no other crime than to be under your orders . . . what is the law that says that the black man must belong to and be the property of the white man? . . . We are your equals then, by natural right, and if nature pleases itself to diversify colours within the human race, it is not a crime to be born black nor an advantage to be white.[44]

The letter praised the French Revolution, 'the fortunate revolution . . . which has opened for us the road which our courage and labour will enable us to ascend, to arrive at the temple of liberty, like those brave Frenchmen who are our models and whom all the universe is contemplating.'[45] But it then proceeded to castigate the colonial assembly for failing to put the great ideals of the French Revolution into practice:

You, gentlemen, who pretend to subject us to slavery – have you not sworn to uphold the French Constitution? What does it say, this respectable constitution? What is the fundamental law? Have you forgotten that you have formally vowed the Declaration of the Rights of Man, which says that men are born free, equal in their rights; that their natural rights include liberty, property, security and resistance to oppression? So then, as you cannot deny what you have sworn, we are within our rights, and you ought to recognise yourselves as perjurers; by your decrees you recognise that all men are free, but you want to maintain servitude for 480,000 individuals who allow you to enjoy all that you possess. Through your envoys you offer liberty only to our chiefs; it is still one of your maxims of politics to say that those who have played an equal part in our work should be delivered by us to be your victims. No, we prefer a thousand deaths to acting that way towards our own kind. If you want to accord us the benefits that are due to us, they must also shower onto all of our brothers . . . [46]

The rebel leaders then demanded 'general liberty for all men detained in slavery', a 'general amnesty for the past' and, if these were accepted, the leaders of the insurgency promised to 'lay down our arms' and 'return to the plantation to which he belongs and resume his work on condition of a wage which will be set by the year for each cultivator who starts work for a fixed term'. We are, they concluded again, 'resolved to live free or die'.[47] This letter testified to the general new feeling of confidence and empowerment among the black masses across Saint-Domingue as a result of the slave revolt. Even in those areas where the revolt had not yet impacted, such as Port-au-Prince, a lack of 'respect' of the enslaved towards white planters was noted. As one planter noted, 'The magic [of racism] has disappeared, how will we replace it?'[48]

The French Revolution Radicalises

In mid-1792, the French Revolution was, in James's words 'still in the hands of Liberals and "moderates"', and 'clearly bent on driving the blacks back to the old slavery'.[49] The dominant thinking among the leaders of the French Revolution at this time was best summed up by the President of the Colonial Assembly at the time: 'We have not brought half-a-million slaves from the coasts of Africa to make them into French citizens.'[50] Yet events were moving fast in France, as the revolution was radicalised amidst the growing dangers of counter-revolutionary restoration, and on 10 August 1792 the Parisian *sans culottes* rose to smash the power of the Bourbon monarchy completely. In January 1793, Louis XVI was executed, and soon the French Revolutionary government under the leadership of the Jacobins found themselves soon at war with Spain, and then England and Holland, as, in James's words, 'the ruling classes of Europe armed against this new monster – democracy'.[51]

The revolutionary struggle against slavery underway in Saint-Domingue was now seen more clearly than ever as an opportunity for European imperial rivals of France – above all Britain and Spain – not just to offer assistance in order to strike a blow against France, but to hijack events in order to capture this valuable colony for themselves. The British took advantage of a long-standing offer by sections of the white planter class of Saint-Domingue to prepare the sending of a force with the aim of re-colonising the colony for the British Empire, knowing that in future it would be very difficult for Republican France to send any troops to the Caribbean when they were needed to fight at home. In early 1793, the Spanish Empire, which had long hoped to regain the colony it had lost a century before, and long supported the black insurgency, now offered the black revolutionaries a formal alliance backed up with guns and supplies to make war on France, and guaranteeing their liberty, some land and other rewards. The black revolutionaries had been beaten regularly for several months by this stage by the better equipped and organised French, who had been freshly reinforced by the arrival of some 6,000 troops from France in 1792. Forced to retreat into the mountains, the black rebels accepted, bringing over about 10,000 much needed soldiers to replenish the Spanish forces as auxiliaries by June 1793.[52]

With a residual loyalty to the king of France and to kingship in general no doubt still in the back of their minds, Jean-François and Biassou became lieutenants-generals of the armies of the king of Spain. Toussaint however slowly began to exercise more autonomy under Biassou, becoming a colonel in his own right, commanding his personally trained elite force of about 600 fighters. Sometime in May or June 1793, Toussaint – less trusting of the slave-holding Spanish than other black rebel leaders – made a covert approach to French General Étienne Laveaux, but no agreement was reached between them that might have seen Toussaint switch sides.[53]

The black insurgents, fortified now by the Spanish, controlled a wide liberated zone across the mountains of the Northern Plain from the important sea port around Gonaïves in the West – where Toussaint himself was based – through to the area around Grand Boucon (where Biassou had his headquarters) and further to the East and closest to the Spanish around Ounaminthe (where Jean-François had his base).[54] Cap Français was isolated and vulnerable, and when the French now began to find themselves increasingly unable to hold their positions against both the black insurgents, on the one hand, and white counter-revolutionary forces, on the other, they began to change tack. When the French civil commissioners Léger Félicité Sonthonax and Étienne Polverel had first arrived in Saint-Domingue in September 1792, they had declared that 'they only knew of two classes of men, free ones and slaves', and that slavery was a necessity for cultivation and economic growth.[55] Now, on 20 June 1793, Sonthonax and Polverel had released a proclamation, which in part declared 'that the will of the French Republic and of its delegates is to give freedom to all the Negro warriors who will fight for the Republic under the orders of the civil commissioners, against Spain or other enemies . . . All the slaves declared free by the delegates of the Republic will be equal to all free men – they will enjoy all the rights belonging to French citizens.'[56]

The proclamation of 20 June 1793 threatened to profoundly reshape hierarchies around race and class in colonial Saint-Domingue because of its implications above all for the free people of colour, and indeed the remaining black population that were still in slavery. It led immediately to what has been described as 'the journée of June 20, 1793' in Cap Français, which began as a struggle between two rival white groups – both fighting in the name of the French Revolution – one of which was supported by the city's free people of colour, and ended with an intervention by the black insurgents themselves. Over the course of three days, fighting destroyed the wealthiest port in the French colonies, leaving perhaps up to 10,000 dead in what Jeremy D. Popkin calls 'the most murderous instance of urban conflict in the entire history of the Americas'.[57]

Toussaint Bréda's reply to the civil commissioner's radical proclamation of 20 June 1793 was typical of the rebel leaders' feelings at this time, 'the blacks wanted to serve under a king and the Spanish king offered his protection'.[58] It was a reflection in part of genuine feelings about the execution of Louis XVI by the 'godless Republic' of France which, despite proclamations about liberty and equality since 1789, had sent thousands of troops to defend slavery in colonies like Saint-Domingue, but also of the growing sense of security and power felt by the black insurgents who after almost two years of fighting still found themselves in control of large sections of the North. Indeed, as Popkin notes, in the aftermath of the *journée* of 20 June 1793 and the end of white control over one of the main colonial ports, 'it became clear that the French revolutionary government would not be able to defeat the slave insurrection', and also 'apparent for the first time that victory for the insurgents might be achieved in alliance with the French, rather than by struggle against them'.[59] As the United States was hit by its first refugee crisis in the aftermath of the *journée*, Thomas Jefferson, then US Secretary of State, noted to James Monroe on 14 July 1793, 'I become daily more and more convinced that all the West India islands will remain in the hands of the people of colour, and a total expulsion of the whites sooner or later take place . . .'.[60] There was also a noticeable radicalisation taking place in the French Republican zone on the question of slavery. As Nick Nesbitt notes, 'with the increasing success of the slave revolt, free citizens, including many whites, were already calling openly for "les Droits de l'Homme" and "liberté générale" as a means of rallying the slaves to fight for the Republic', and 'on August 24, 15,000 free men voted for the emancipation of the slaves in the North of the island'.[61]

The Emergence of Toussaint Louverture

This changing situation on the Republican side did not pass unnoticed by Toussaint Bréda, who now publicly cast off his old name and adopted the new name 'Louverture', 'the opening'. On 25 August 1793, 'Toussaint Louverture' explicitly addressed the free coloured Republicans in a letter. Hailing them his 'brothers and friends', he argued that blacks like himself fighting for the Spanish were already fighting for 'general liberty'. 'The idea of this general liberty for which you are fighting your friends, who was it who established the basis of it, aren't I the original author?' Threatening that the Spanish forces were soon going 'to strike a great blow against all the enemies of peace', he suggested it would be best for them to 'join our side' before then. 'We have begun, have been able to hold firm, and having begun I will finish. Who threatens with the sword will die by the sword'.[62] As Nick Nesbitt notes, 'the impressive fact is that Toussaint already possessed, in this his first public statement, a *logic* of universal rights whose scope of address was not a class or race, but all humanity.'[63] On 27 August 1793, Louverture followed up this letter with another, written on behalf of the Spanish king's armies to again reiterate the Spanish armies' disgust at the execution of Louis XVI:

> Perfidious republicans! . . . You tell us that triumphant France is sensitive to our suffering and sends us representatives to protect us . . . what misleading lies! Crime and carnage reign in France and a great king is needed to save the state . . . as long as God gives us strength and the means, we will obtain another freedom, different from the one you tyrants want to impose on us.[64]

Such ideas of kingship still carried considerable weight among many black insurgents, and one Kongo-born figure, Macaya, who had been sent as an emissary to Jean-François and Biassou by Sonthonax and Polverel, would soon decide to go over to the Spanish camp. As Macaya put it when an attempt was made to persuade him to rejoin the Republican forces,

> I am the subject of three kings: of the King of Congo, master of all the blacks; of the King of France who represents my father; of the King of Spain who represents my mother. These three Kings are the descendants of those who, led by a star, came to adore God made man. If I went over to the Republic, I might be forced to make war against my brothers, the subjects of these three kings to whom I have promised loyalty.[65]

Yet with his talk of obtaining 'another freedom', Louverture, though writing as a Spanish officer and 'General of the royal armies', was also clearly responding to Sonthonax's June proclamation and making an intervention in defining the meaning of 'freedom' in more radical terms than it was being posed by the French Republicans.

On 29 August 1793, Sonthonax, recognising the *de facto* reality of abolition at the hands of the black insurgents just two years after their insurrection had begun, formally proclaimed the end of slavery for those 'currently enslaved' in the North Province (the area under his control). Sonthonax's edict explicitly citing *The Declaration of the Rights of Man and the Citizen* began by noting that 'Men are born free and live free and equal in rights'. More radically still, Sonthonax noted the former enslaved masses would 'enjoy all the rights attached to the quality of French citizenship', without the whip or even any notion of a period of 'apprenticeship' between slavery and freedom, as the most enlightened *philosophes* on the question of slavery such as Condorcet thought essential.[66]

Nonetheless, for Sonthonax, 'freedom' was to be understood as a 'gift' from France, and would be understood and interpreted through the French system of law and order. Forced labour would remain, with Article 9 noting that 'slaves currently attached to the plantations of their former masters will be obliged to remain there and to work the land', instead of developing as independent small farmers, and lighter forms of punishment such as imprisonment, loss of pay or 'one to three days in the stocks' used to discipline the formerly enslaved.[67] As Sonthonax put it while explaining his proclamation to a huge crowd,

> Never forget . . . that of all the whites in the universe, only the French of Europe are your friends . . . Do not believe that the liberty you are about to enjoy is a state of laziness and idleness. In France, everyone is free and everyone works. In Saint Domingue, under the same laws, you will follow the same example.[68]

In issuing his historic 'emancipation proclamation', Sonthonax was in part honouring his early principled opposition to slavery as a young lawyer inspired by the ideals of the French Revolution before arriving in Saint-Domingue, and in part clearly hoping that this would finally win the black armies and its leaders away from the slave-owning Spanish empire to the side of the French. It certainly gave many blacks fighting with the Spanish – not least Louverture himself – much to ponder.[69] A few, like Barthélemy, the insurgent leader in the Limbé parish, did now come over to the French, declaring that 'Spain is trying to maintain slavery, not to free slaves'.[70] However, it was unclear whether Sonthonax was acting with the full knowledge and approval of the French Republican government in Paris, and – more critically at this stage – also unclear how long that government might itself last, given that France was now besieged by counter-revolutionary armies in Europe, even if it did ratify Sonthonax's decision.[71]

The same day as Sonthonax's proclamation, Louverture – in all likelihood writing unaware of the details of the historic edict being declared by Sonthonax, even if he could sense the way the ideological wind was blowing in the French Republican zone – was again also reiterating his own complete commitment to the abolition of slavery in another letter addressed to Republican free coloured fighters from his headquarters on the Turel plantation:

Brothers and Friends,

I can only groan at the state in which you have been plunged for so long and at the misfortune that might occur after you have persisted with such unity in defending laws that can offer no more than an apparent happiness, but which you believe to be very real. You do not know the person who is addressing you. Be assured that he is a true brother who thinks and can see that you are among enemies without realising it. Goodness, integrity, and humanity are the foundation of our characters. The wise advice I am giving you will leave you no doubt of it.

. . . I am Toussaint Louverture. You have perhaps heard of my name. You are aware, brothers, that I have undertaken this vengeance, and that I want freedom and equality to reign in Saint Domingue. I have been working since the beginning to bring it into existence to establish the happiness of all of us. But alas! You unfortunately cannot see it. Look at yourselves. Look well at the character of those leading you. Open your eyes and you will see, first and foremost, manipulators, untrustworthy men who seek only to destroy all of you . . . You do not know what state France is in. They can't give you any news except what they make up to support their party . . .

I have to mention the question of our fighting. You say you are fighting for liberty and equality? Is it possible that we are tearing each other apart for one and the same cause? It is I who have taken this on and want to fight for them until they are established and recognized among us. You want nothing of that, being our enemy. Equality cannot exist without liberty, and for liberty to exist we need unity . . . .

Toussaint Louverture, General of the armies for the public good.[72]

Whether he knew of Sonthonax's proclamation or not, this statement – and the others from him written around this time discussing the need for general emancipation – certainly challenged Sonthonax's claim to be the true apostle of liberty locally. They also began to clearly distinguish Louverture from other black leaders such as Jean-François and Biassou, who according to some reports for their own personal ends had long been rounding up 'troublemakers' in their own ranks to be sold into slavery to the Spanish.[73] In terms of rhetoric, Louverture was following the customary pattern of invoking both the cause of human rights and universal claims of *The Declaration of the Rights of Man and the Citizen* and the 'public good', as well as the authority and prestige which came from his position as a general in the 'Armies of the King'. However, Louverture's supreme confidence in the idea of winning 'liberty' and these rights through struggle from below was manifest in this statement, and as Bell notes, 'he who eighteen months before would have put the slaves back into harness for fifty liberties was now and henceforward completely, fervently committed to liberty for all the blacks of Saint Domingue'.[74]

Nonetheless Louverture's position was not without any contradictions, and his continuing loyalty to the Spanish king in his letters was met with a response from the Republican side, with a local commander who had already come over to the army of 'brave French citizens of all colours without distinction', Bramante Lazzary, noting on 30 August 1793 that now 'general liberty has been proclaimed on the island', the French flag – the tricolour – now 'makes it clear that our liberty depends on these three colours; white, mulatto, black'. 'We are fighting for these three colours. The nobility and the Spaniards want us to have only the white in order to bring us back to the old order. But no, we are French; we are fighting for our freedom; we want to live free or die, that is the motto of all good French republicans.'[75]

Lazzary sent a copy of Sonthonax's proclamation directly to Louverture the same day, and in an accompanying letter, he suggested that God was more likely to act against Louverture as them, for 'without the error that Spanish barbarism and slavery has thrown you into, Saint-Domingue would already be peaceful and would enjoy the same happiness.'

> There are no more slaves in Saint-Domingue; all men of all colours are free and equal in their rights and believe this is the greatest of gifts. What have you received from the time of kings for centuries for your work and your natural virtues . . . Remember above all that all good Frenchmen shudder at the word king, who you must know were never happy unless they were surrounded by slaves, and since the twenty-first of January our motherland no longer has one and enjoys perfect happiness. We are her children and of the same opinion and will all die rather than recognize tyrants and their ferocious imitators. We all have as our motto 'to live free or die' and will prove it to you when you give us the chance.[76]

Yet Louverture was not willing to give the French that chance, and his decision to change his name from Bréda in August 1793 is perhaps not only symbolic of his new-found commitment to 'general liberty', but also suggestive as to why this was the case. It has been claimed in one 1796 account by Jean-Philippe Garran 'that he got the name *the Opening* from his facility in creating conciliatory openings', and this makes some sense from a French perspective given their relatively long lines of communication and dialogue with him.[77] It has also been claimed that it derives from Polverel's reaction to Toussaint's military genius, not least his by now manifest ability to move with lightning speed across the region of the West where he was based, enabling him to give leadership and direction at critical battles and skirmishes. As Polverel is said to have admiringly noted after Toussaint captured

Dondon and Marmelade for the Spanish in 1793, 'Ce bougre-là se fait donc ouverture partout!' – 'That man makes an opening everywhere!' Ralph Korngold noted that it also marked a desire within Toussaint to raise his profile as a leader among the black insurgents. Rather than risk being associated forever with someone who had remained on the Bréda plantation during the August 1791 insurrection, the new name meant there was a very good chance 'Toussaint Louverture' would now be forever associated with those who had made 'the opening', and that he had indeed worked 'since the beginning' for liberty and equality. 'Oh, you Africans, my brothers', Louverture would later declare, 'have you forgotten that it is I who first raised the standard of insurrection against tyranny, against the despotism that kept you in chains?'[78]

Yet Korngold also noted a more 'subtle significance' to the name, given the beloved Vodou god Legba, the spirit of gates and crossroads and indeed the keeper (and also opener) of the Gate of Destiny. A popular chant in creole at the start of Vodou ceremonies was 'Papa Legba, ouvri barriè pour moins' – 'Papa Legba, open the gate for me!' Louverture, despite his personal Catholicism and even hostility towards Vodou at certain points of his career, was no doubt mindful of the advantage that would inevitably come with making a spiritual association with such a powerful figure as Papa Legba.[79] Such a subtle appeal to the mentality of the enslaved masses also further helped Louverture distinguish his call for liberty from that of Sonthonax and the French, whom he still distrusted.[80] As he had put it in his letter on 27 August 1793, 'we will obtain another freedom, different from the one [that the French] want to impose on us'.[81] He did not see freedom like Lazzary, as 'the greatest of gifts' bestowed by the French, but rather as something that had to be fought and won by the enslaved themselves. In short, the adoption of the name 'Louverture' strengthened his voice in the battle to define the contested meaning of liberty in Saint-Domingue, and accordingly, as Korngold notes, was 'a stroke of genius on the part of Toussaint, and undoubtedly contributed towards his success'.[82]

3

Black Jacobin Ascending:
1793–98

The revolutionary upheaval in Saint-Domingue, together with the outbreak of war in Europe in February 1793, had given not only the Spanish but also their imperial rivals the British an incredible opportunity to attempt to seize one of the world's richest sugar colonies and restore the highly-profitable business of slavery. Henry Dundas, home secretary in William Pitt's first administration (and soon to become secretary of state for war and colonies) had already been in negotiations with a number of counter-revolutionary planters from Saint-Domingue to agree that the British Empire might assume protection of the 'Queen of the Antilles' in case of war with France.[1] As early as September 1793, one month after Sonthonax's historic decree abolishing slavery, the first 600 red-coated British troops arriving from Jamaica had already disembarked at the tiny port of Jérémie on the southern peninsula. The tiny number of invading foreign troops were greeted there and – a few days later, more significantly – at the great naval fort in the northwest, Môle Saint-Nicolas, 'the Gibraltar of the Antilles', by local white planters and troops, who happily defected and relinquished their positions with the refrain 'Vivent les Anglais!' – 'Long live the English!'[2]

Ships full of reinforcements for this invasion force began to be assembled in Britain in preparation to sail across the Atlantic, and port cities along the West coast of Saint-Domingue slowly began to fall one by one into the hands of the British forces already there; but one ship that now left Saint-Domingue to brave an Atlantic crossing while France was at war with Britain, the greatest naval power in earth, was ultimately, perhaps, to be of more historic significance.

In September 1793, the besieged French Republicans in Cap Français had elected – in what Geggus notes was 'the first multiracial election in France's colonies' – a delegation to carry the news of Sonthonax and Polverel's emancipation proclamation across the Atlantic to the National Convention in Paris.[3] The three-strong delegation from Saint-Domingue, which eventually made it to Paris in February 1794, was composed of Jean-Baptiste Belley (an African-born officer who, like Louverture, had been both enslaved and slave owner), Jean-Baptiste-Mills (a member of the free-coloured population) and Louis Dufay (a white delegate). The trio made an immediate impact when they entered the Convention to applause. One deputy, Camboulas, rose to declare that 'since 1789 the aristocracy of birth and the aristocracy of religion have been destroyed; but the aristocracy of the skin still remains. That too is now at its last gasp, and equality has been consecrated'. Camboulas continued, 'a black, a yellow, and a white have taken their seat among us, in the name of the free citizens of Saint-Domingue'.[4]

The next day, 4 February 1794 (16 Pluviôse an II), the National Convention in revolutionary France – under the control of the Jacobins and with public detestation of racism, 'the aristocracy of the skin', rising in crescendo in France itself – voted not simply to ratify Sonthonax's emancipation proclamation, but to abolish slavery throughout the French empire.[5] 'The National Convention declares that slavery is abolished throughout the territory of the Republic; in consequence all men, without distinction of colour, will enjoy the right of French citizens.' The formerly enslaved delegate Belley was so moved he vowed, 'on behalf of my brothers', that the tricolour flag 'that has called us to our liberty' will fly in Saint-Domingue 'as long as there is a drop of blood in our veins'.[6] Amid the general exaltation, the French revolutionary leader Georges Danton foresaw the potential profound implications for the revolutionary struggle that this historic decree represented, and triumphantly proclaimed: 'Representatives of the French people, until now we have decreed liberty as egotists for ourselves. But today we proclaim universal liberty . . . Today the Englishman is dead! [Loud applause] Pitt and his plots are done for!'[7]

Meanwhile back in Saint-Domingue, matters were finely and delicately balanced between the three competing military power blocs. The British army was close to occupying about a third of France's richest colony after its first eight months of invasion, with minimal losses and minimum effort on their part, and in June 1794 (with the help of long awaited reinforcements) would finally take Port-au-Prince in the south.[8] Yet the actual number of effective combat forces at the disposal of the British was very low – certainly still under one thousand men in spring 1794 – and these were seriously overstretched and suffering from falling morale, as well as overly dependent on the increasingly questionable loyalty of local white colonists. In late April 1794, the local commander of the British forces, Sir Adam Williamson, wrote to Dundas to insist on the urgent need for reinforcements as his operation had come to a standstill due to lack of men, and he now feared local colonists rebelling in the occupied territories.[9]

Another problem the British (and white European troops in general) would encounter soon enough was their lack of immunity to diseases like yellow fever and malaria. Their arrival in the midst of a tropical summer – the sickly season – could not have been worse timing. Even though the British had captured Port-au-Prince in June 1794, within just two months 650 soldiers in this mosquito-ridden port town with poor sanitation and swampy terrain would be dead. The British garrison at Port-au-Prince had been all but annihilated, the result not of combat, but simply from infectious diseases.[10] 'They dropt', one British observer noted, 'like leaves in the autumn.'[11]

The French Republicans were embattled, but still held a reasonable amount of territory outside Cap Français and Port-de-Paix, their heavily defended 'boulevards of liberty' in the North. Sonthonax – guessing and gambling that the Convention would indeed ratify his abolition decree – was determinedly and actively trying to recruit bands of insurgent black rebels wherever possible into the recently formed *Légion de l'Égalité*.[12] While Polverel remained close to the more conservative free people of colour, Sonthonax championed the newly freed citizens of his 29 August 'emancipation proclamation', calling for guerrilla warfare and a scorched earth strategy to avoid the victory of the slave-holding empires of Britain or Spain.

Let us unite, citizens, to push back the forces of slavery and death. Unite, men of April 4 and August 29: the same fate threatens all of you. They will put you in irons. Swear to die rather than to accept them; can you not retreat to your hills and forests [to continue the fight]?[13]

As Sonthonax wrote to Polverel, 'let buildings perish rather than have them cemented with the blood of the men of colour and the Africans. Let plantations perish a thousand times rather than see them worked again by slaves.' Polverel however felt that the former enslaved ultimately needed to be back at work on privately owned plantations if freedom was to have any long-term chance of success in Saint-Domingue, and responded with a warning to Sonthonax that 'you are devoted to fire'. Witnessing the Republican position slowly worsening, Sonthonax impatiently shot back to his fellow commissioner, 'when one is far from the scene of action, one always judges it badly. It is very easy for you, surrounded by a legion of 2,400 men to . . . censure my operations.'[14]

For their part, the Spanish were cautious about leaving the frontier of Santo Domingo undefended, and so before May 1794 had not launched the kind of major offensive in Saint-Domingue that so many were anticipating. David Geggus notes that the Spanish were in a more precarious situation than is often realised, and were massively dependent on their black auxiliary troops:

Even after substantial reinforcements arrived in March 1794, it is unlikely there were ever more than 3,500 Spanish troops in the whole island. Dogged by disease, they were always outnumbered by the republicans. Utterly immobile, refusing to cooperate with the British, they reluctantly relied on their black allies (*troupes auxiliaries*) to do their fighting for them. The auxiliaries, however, spent much of their time feuding with one another.[15]

Here we return to Louverture, who – despite being personally responsible for half the military advances secured by the Spanish north of the River Artibonite in the West, including capturing the town of Gonaïves in December 1793 – was also bogged down in bloody feuds with his immediate Spanish superior Juan de Lleonart. Lleonart had chosen to defend the higher-ranking general Biassou, even though Biassou had raided Louverture's supplies and sold the wives and children of Louverture's troops into slavery.[16] There was also growing dissent and a number of revolts among blacks working on Spanish controlled plantations, especially in early 1794 after white planters under Spanish protection reintroduced whipping.[17] The Spanish support for slavery added to the growing dissatisfaction among Spanish black auxiliary troops, including Louverture, while the free people of colour who had sided with the Spanish and British were also increasingly questioning their loyalties. Defections to the Republican side were growing.[18]

Louverture's Volte-face

In May 1794, as rumours of the historic passing in France of the decree of 16 Pluviôse an II (4 February 1794) slowly began to filter into Saint-Domingue, and after a personal letter of invitation from the French general Etienne Laveaux on 5 May of the same year, Louverture made his famous yet complex *volte-face* as he defected from the Spanish to join the French. Louverture's reputation for humanitarianism and discipline (in stark comparison with other Spanish generals like Biassou and Jean-François) meant the forces under his direct disposal had by now grown massively. If Louverture had had about 600 troops at the start of his campaign against the French Republicans, he now had some 4,000, including several excellent and important officers like Henri Christophe, Hyacinthe Moïse (his adopted nephew) and Jean-Jacques Dessalines. Louverture raised the tricolour over Gonaïves, and ensured the whole area in the North Province under his command – Gros-Morne, Ennery, Marmelade, Plaisance, Dondon, Acul and Limbé – was now integrated into the French Republican camp, all in all a massive blow to the Spanish, and also a new potential threat to British power.[19]

On 18 May 1794, Louverture, now General of the Western Army, wrote to Laveaux, the interim Governor-General, to account for his previous decision to fight with the Spanish. 'It is true, General, that I have been led into error by the enemies of the Republic and humanity, but what man can flatter himself to have avoided all the traps of evil men?' Louverture declared that 'you will remember that . . . my goal was only that we unite to combat the enemies of France and to bring to an end the internal war among the French of this colony. Unfortunately for all concerned, the paths toward reconciliation that I suggested were rejected.'[20] After apparently being 'abandoned by the French, my brothers', Louverture had turned to the Spanish who 'offered me their protection and freedom for all who fought for the cause of kings'.

But a somewhat late experience opened my eyes to these perfidious protectors. Having perceived their treachery, I saw clearly that they intended for us to set upon each other to diminish our number and to enchain those who remained to return them to their former slavery. No, never would they achieve their infamous goal! And we will have revenge on these contemptible beings in our turn in every way. Let us unite forever, therefore, and, forgetting the past, let us seek henceforth only to crush our enemies and to avenge ourselves against our treacherous neighbours.[21]

On 24 May 1794, Laveaux could report to Polverel that 'Toussaint Louverture, one of the three chiefs of the African royalists, in coalition with the Spanish Government, had at last discovered his true interests and that of his brothers; he has realised that kings can never be the friends of liberty; he fights today for the Republic at the head of an armed force.'[22] Sonthonax and Polverel enthusiastically welcomed their newest recruit, and sent Louverture a personal greeting stressing their own republicanism.

The French Republic wants liberty. Kings breathe only slavery. Black kings on the Guinea coast sell unhappy Africans to whites. White kings send the ships to carry them to Saint Domingue . . . Therefore, citizen, bless the National Assembly which, in overthrowing the thrones of kings, has based the happiness of man on equality and liberty . . . Those, citizen, are our principles. To uphold them, we have braved poisons and daggers.[23]

Louverture's dramatic, radical political shift from royalism to republicanism may have had other more ulterior motives than those he had stated to Laveaux, but, as David Geggus notes, it was nonetheless 'a decisive turning point in the Haitian Revolution . . . Black militancy and the libertarian ideology of the French Revolution were now melded, and the cause of slave emancipation had found a leader of genius'.[24] Louverture's letter had a characteristic regret for the 'few unfortunate whites who were victims' after he routed the Spanish forces from the area under his control. 'I am utterly unlike many others who witness scenes of horror in cold blood. I have always held humanity in common to all, and I suffer whenever I cannot prevent evil.' Louverture was also keen to show himself a responsible figure to be trusted by Laveaux as he stressed his willingness to defend the new order and impose discipline both in the army and on the war-ravaged plantations in the areas under his control. 'There were also a number of uprisings in the workshops, but I rapidly returned things to order and all are working as before.'[25]

Defeating the Spanish

By the summer of 1794, thanks in no small part to Louverture, while Spanish and British forces still occupied territory in the east, Republican forces had defeated the Spanish in the west. On 7 July 1794, having just defeated the rebel leader Jean-François's Spanish forces in Dondon, Louverture again wrote to Laveaux. Louverture noted that Jean-François had attacked his troops at Port Margot, 'but he was always repulsed vigorously' until Louverture was in a position to strike back.

Having taken my bearings, I attacked simultaneously Dondon, the Fort [Dauphin], and other posts. These were taken sabre in hand. I very nearly captured Jean-François; he owed his salvation to the thickness of the bushes he threw himself into in desperation, leaving his clothes behind him. I captured all his affairs and papers. He saved only his shirt and pants. My troops made a carnage of his men and I took many prisoners . . . [26]

Writing as a 'servant of the Republic', Louverture also noted to Laveaux that he had received a printed version of the National Convention's abolition decree of 16 Pluviôse an II, describing the resolution as 'reassuring news for friends of humanity, and I hope that in the future all will feel more at ease and that, if we are able to enjoy peace and tranquillity, the colony will flourish to an unparalleled degree . . .'[27] Unfortunately, 'peace and tranquillity' were not immediate options for Saint-Domingue, and after Sonthonax and Polverel were recalled to Paris to face charges from the exiled planters for their emancipation decree, Laveaux was left in charge to face the Spanish and British without aid or assistance from revolutionary France.[28] Louverture, and his disciplined but poor, hungry and ill-equipped black soldiers, would now become critical to the survival not only of the French Republicans in Saint-Domingue, but also the besieged French Republic itself.

Louverture now went on the offensive against the Spanish-held positions in the east, and in October 1794, with effective use of cavalry, captured the inland towns of Saint-Michel and Saint-Raphael, burning them to the ground rather than trying to hold them. This was something previous Republican generals had previously found impossible, and by late December 1794, Louverture had succeeded in surrounding and defeating Jean-François's 3,000 strong army through an elaborate and sophisticated pincer movement, with several columns under the leadership of Dessalines and Moïse securing the Grande-Rivière region.[29] As David Geggus notes, 'Toussaint Louverture, by these victories, brought large quantities of artillery, cash and ammunition into Republican hands and established himself as a brilliant commander . . . [he] now led a victorious and well-supplied army. He commanded some thirty camps in a cordon that stretched nearly ninety miles and had built up an officer corps of talent and experience, consisting mainly of blacks'.[30]

Both Jean-François and Louverture were also by now engaged in a bitter and desperate battle of ideas to win the hearts and minds of black fighters for the Spanish crown and French Republic respectively. In a letter to his 'brothers' on the Republican side, Jean-François – whose forces by early 1795 had been reduced to just a thousand or so fighters, after being almost 7,000 strong in 1793 –

warned that the French former masters could not be trusted. 'The liberty the Republicans tell you about is false', and once France had secured a European peace Jean-François argued that 'they will arm convoys that will be full of white soldiers, who will reduce you to a state of servitude'.³¹ For Louverture, however, as he wrote in a reply to Jean-François on 13 June 1795, it was not the Republicans who had offered the blacks liberty, for as Republicans, 'we are free by natural right'. 'It could only be kings, whose name alone expresses what is most vile and despicable, who could dare claim the right to reduce into servitude men made like them and whom nature has made free'.³²

Louverture proudly now put his republicanism into action, overseeing with the support of Dessalines and a black 'battalion of sansculottes' a great victory over a famous royalist white Creole corps made up of old planters under Dessource in June 1795. As Louverture described his military strategy to Laveaux, '[t]he enemy had not taken the precaution to establish on the St Marc road reserve camps to protect his retreat', enabling Louverture to surround Dessource's army and use 'a trick to encourage him to pass by the highway'. Louverture put himself at the head of the cavalry, and they kept Dessource's forces 'busy' while Louverture's two columns of infantry moved into position on either flank of the highway backed up with cannon.

> As soon as these two columns arrived within pistol shot, I served the enemy in true republican fashion. He [Dessource] continued his way showing all the time a brave front. But the first cannon shot that I caused to be fired among his men, and which did a great deal of damage, made him abandon first a wagon and then a piece of cannon. I redoubled the charge and afterwards I captured the other three pieces of cannon, two wagons full of munitions, and seven others full of wounded who were promptly sent to the rear. Then it was that the enemy began to fly in the greatest disorder, only for those at the head of the retreat to find themselves right in the mouth of the piece of cannon which I had posted at Detroit on the Moreau plantation. And when the enemy saw himself taken in front, behind, and on all sides, that fine fellow, the impertinent Dessources [*sic*], jumped off his horse and threw himself into the

brushwood with the debris of his army calling out 'Every man for himself'. Rain and darkness caused me to discontinue the pursuit. This battle lasted from eleven in the morning to six in the evening and cost me only six dead and as many wounded. I have strewn the road with corpses for the distance of more than a league. My victory has been most complete and if the celebrated Dessources [*sic*] is lucky enough to re-enter St Marc it will be without cannon, without baggage, in short what is called with neither drum nor trumpet. He has lost everything, even honour, if vile royalists are capable of having any. He will remember for a long time the republican lesson which I have taught him.[33]

In October 1795, Louverture and Moïse united their forces – who threw themselves into battle under the slogan 'Long live the Republic!' – to successively repel a Spanish counter-offensive by Biassou and Jean-François in what would prove a particularly bloody battle. In Europe, however, the Spanish had already conceded defeat to the French and signed the Treaty of Basel. News of this was slow to reach Saint-Domingue, but when it did, it brought fighting to an end. Biassou and Jean-François now left Saint-Domingue under Spanish protection, the former ultimately to retire to Florida while the latter would live in mainland Spain for many years. Though in a sense defeated by Louverture, as Geggus notes, Biassou and Jean-François achieved what they set out to personally accomplish for they never really aimed at 'citizenship', but rather 'amnesty for their followers and freedom for themselves and their families to keep their booty and settle elsewhere'.[34] Louverture, finally breathing a sigh of relief at the news of the departure of his one-time fellow black insurgent leaders, turned rivals and enemies, wrote to Laveaux in November 1795: 'Praise be to God, Jean-François is going to leave.'[35]

Defeating the British

Before playing a central role in routing the Spanish forces, during the summer and autumn of 1794, Louverture had laid siege to the well-fortified western British garrison at Saint Marc from his base in Gonaïves, through a sophisticated mixture of subtle subterfuge.

This sparked an internal mutiny against the British in the port itself, which was followed up with a conventional military assault. The British, under the determined Major Thomas Brisbane, managed to fend off the Republican forces until the arrival of reinforcements, including a frigate which bombarded Louverture's troops from the sea.[36] The British were also helped by the loyalty of their free coloured auxiliaries, and also in part – according to Louverture himself – because he had recently crushed his hand helping move a cannon and so was unable to lead the assault himself. 'If I had been able to fight as I usually do at the head of my troops the enemy would not have held an hour, or else I would have died, one or the other.'[37] As Korngold notes, in all his campaigns Louverture 'gave evidence of physical courage that bordered on recklessness . . . in the course of his military career he was wounded seventeen times, but never seriously. He led a charmed life. Imagine a man being hit in the face by a spent cannon ball and escaping with the loss of a few teeth!'[38]

The British everywhere were finding themselves on the back foot, besieged by French Republican forces – not only by black troops commanded by the likes of Louverture, but also free coloured fighters under inspired and courageous generals like André Rigaud in the south and Louis-Jacques Bauvais in the west. The British were increasingly dependent on their own free coloured and black auxiliary troops, who were increasingly wavering in their loyalty if not openly mutinous, and wondering if fighting with the British was the best hope to ensure their freedom and rights.[39] By the end of 1794, the British regular army – still only about 1,100 strong – were isolated in four distinct coastal patches – around Môle Saint-Nicolas, around Saint Marc, the region around Port-au-Prince itself, and finally in the south La Grande Anse, the area around Jérémie and Irois – and cut off from communication with each other except by sea.[40] As Jean-Baptiste Belley, who had since 1794 been based in Paris representing Saint-Domingue in the National Convention, put it in 1795:

I . . . attest that, if the English failed to take over all of Saint-Domingue, it is because the blacks who have become free and French have made a rampart with their bodies against this invasion and are bravely defending the rights of the republic. It is certain that if these brave patriots had arms and ammunition, the undeserving blood of the English and the planter traitors would water this land that has been dirtied by their presence for too long.[41]

In July 1795, Pitt and his ministers – above all his secretary of state for war and colonies Henry Dundas – decided that what was needed was not to cut their losses and end the occupation, but rather to launch a new and powerful military expedition to the West Indies under the command of Sir Ralph Abercromby. As David Brion Davis notes,

In the eyes of British leaders, Jacobin and abolitionist principles threatened by 1795 to subvert the entire West Indian world. In Saint-Domingue, Toussaint's ex-slaves had won brilliant victories and were closing in on Britain's disease-ridden troops; armies of former slaves and free coloureds had expelled the British from Guadeloupe and Saint Lucia; racial warfare raged in Grenada and Saint Vincent; French free coloured agents were blamed for inciting a Maroon War in Jamaica.[42]

As Dundas claimed in parliament in February 1796, this was 'not a war for riches or local aggrandisement but a war for security'.[43] From early 1796, the first contingents – some 6,000 cavalry troops of an anticipated deployment of 12,000 reinforcements – accordingly began to land in Saint-Domingue, part of what was (according to Roger Norman Buckley) 'the largest expedition ever to sail from British shores'. It was envisaged and hoped that light cavalry could neutralise the speed of the mobile infantry favoured by generals like Louverture.[44] The routing of the Spanish forces had opened up the possibility for the British to recolonise the once rich slave colony for themselves, and during the summer of 1795, local British forces in Saint-Domingue – with their morale also no doubt boosted by news of coming reinforcements – had felt encouraged enough to try and launch a new offensive heading inland towards the fertile Mirebalais region. Though Louverture managed to keep this latest British advance in check, his poorly equipped army had been forced to adopt a scorched earth strategy, burning plantations and eventually retreating by the autumn of 1795.[45]

The arrival of thousands of newly fresh British troops into Saint-Domingue initially looked like it might change the balance of forces dramatically. From 1795, the British had also developed a strategy of recruiting black troops into newly formed regiments – the 'British Chasseurs' – made up of about 7,000 mainly African-born fighters skilled in guerrilla warfare and recruited from British West Indian colonies with promises of freedom from slavery.[46] In Saint-Domingue, they also cleverly engaged in 'divide-and-rule' tactics, exploiting resentment between the former enslaved and former masters among the French Republican side and playing them off against each other to try and weaken the fragile alliance between free coloured and black. In the south, Rigaud's local leadership was resented by, among others, Pierre Dieudonné, a Kongolese-born commander who controlled an independent band of some 3,000 soldiers in the mountains above Port-au-Prince. Dieudonné had been trusted and admired by Sonthonax, but was bitter at the lack of black officers in Rigaud's army, and so had opened up negotiations with the British, who were hoping to bribe him to switch sides.

On 12 February 1796, Louverture wrote to Dieudonné, whom he had not had the opportunity to meet personally, to try to dissuade him from going over to 'the English', 'the sworn enemies of our freedom and equality' and 'scoundrels who wish to return us to the shameful chains that we had so much difficulty breaking'. 'Is it possible, my dear friend, that in the moment when France has triumphed over all the royalists and . . . grants us all the rights for which we have been fighting, that you would let yourself be deceived by our former tyrants, who only exploit a group of our unfortunate brothers the better to enchain the others?' Louverture stressed that only 'by serving the French Republic' and standing under its flag 'that we are truly free and equal', and so insisted that Rigaud and Bauvais are 'good republicans' and 'our brothers'. Indeed, the French Republic 'is the mother of us all', it 'is one and indivisible', and Louverture reminds his correspondent 'that that is what constitutes its strength, and that it will vanquish all its enemies'.[47] Though Dieudonné was not convinced and refused Louverture's urging to stay loyal to France, this had been anticipated by Louverture who had sent the letter with one of his lieutenants, Laplume. Laplume then led a successful uprising against Dieudonné, and brought Dieudonné's troops under Louverture's control, a great victory though to be slightly pyrrhic. As Dubois notes, 'the tensions that had been smouldering between the coloured officers and the leaders of the "African bands" were not resolved, just transferred into the beginnings of a conflict between Rigaud and Louverture.'⁴⁸

One of those who sailed for Saint-Domingue in February 1796 as part of Abercromby's expedition was Thomas Phipps Howard, a lieutenant in the York Hussars, a unit which consisted of some 80 officers – including non-commissioned officers – and just over 600 men. Howard kept a journal of his time in Saint-Domingue, and, as Buckley notes, 'candidly recorded the defeat of the British forces by a combination of factors, including the heroic and sophisticated resistance of Toussaint's troops'.⁴⁹ In early July 1796, Howard's regiment disembarked into Saint Marc, but 'in about three or four Days after our arrival, the Troops Barracked below [just outside the main gate of Saint Marc] began to feel in the most horrid manner the Plague'.

The putridity of the Disorder at last arose to such an h[e]ight that hundreds, almost, were absolutely drowned in their own Blood, bursting from them at every Pore. Some died raving Mad, others forming Plans for attacking, the others desponding; in fact, Death presented itself under every form an unlimited Imagination could invent. To sum up this Picture of Horror, by a Return made from the 3th July to the 13th, our Regiment alone had lost eight Officers, three Quartermasters, thirteen Serjeants and Corporals, and one hundred & fifty Hussards.⁵⁰

Later in July 1796, when trying to help construct a fort on a mountain overlooking Saint Marc, Howard's troops came under repeated attack, and he describes how, at an hour before daybreak on 22 July, 'the Brigands attacked the Post with at least 1500 or two thousand Men'. The British cannon helped repel the attack but then misfired and became 'totally useless'.

> The three Shots from the Gun stopped the Enemy for some little time. but finding it was not repeated, & judging from thence that some Accident had happened to it, they returned to the Charge with redoubled Ardour; & the musketry was played on both sides with great vigour for nearly two hours, when our Detachment, finding they were not reinforced & having fired away nearly all their Ammunition, [and having also] lost their Commanding Officer who was killed early in the Engagement with two other Officers & the English Serjeant . . . began to retreat down the side of the Mountain . . . the Brigands seeing them retreating in rather a disorderly manner, followed them with a ferocity scarcely to be conceived & absolutely pushed several with their Bayonets down the Mountain . . .[51]

Facing troops who proved themselves to be as organised, courageous, skilled and tactically astute as this, on top of the problems of climate and disease, it is no wonder many British officers on the ground in Saint-Domingue were soon urging caution and even withdrawal rather than get bogged down in terrain where open, conventional warfare was a rarity. 'A British admiral, wishing to give King George III a visual notion of the tortuous topography of Haiti, crumpled up a sheet of paper, threw it upon the table and said: "Sire, Haiti looks like that".'[52] One of the 'men on the spot', Lieutenant Colonel Thomas Maitland, wrote home to his brother in July 1796, noting that Britain had been 'drawn by the folly or misrepresentation of weak interested & inconsiderate men' into a 'labyrinth of Difficulty'. Already, over 6,000 men had been lost and 'all our boasted Army has dwindled to nothing'. As for the security of British fortifications, 'not one post [was] tenable against an enemy in any force . . . You therefore own what you now hold to the forebearance of your Enemy, & not to your own strength.' Military victory over the former enslaved in such circumstances seemed all but impossible, even for a professional army like the British. As Maitland concluded, 'We have no business on that Island', and it was no surprise, having witnessed the black troops in action, that he felt that one possible future was a 'Negroe free Government arising out of the ruins of European Despotism'.[53]

As a result of his ability to reduce European regiments to ruins, one black freeman – Louverture – was certainly rising to hold increasingly powerful positions of government in Saint-Domingue. In recognition of his outstanding achievements on the battlefield and apparent unceasing loyalty to the appointed representatives of revolutionary France in the colony (above all the aristocratic Governor Laveaux), Louverture had steadily risen in prominence from proconsul of the Western Province to then deputy-governor on 1 April 1796. As Laveaux now declared, he would henceforth do nothing without Louverture's approval, and proclaimed Louverture to be not only 'the saviour of the constituted authorities' but also – echoing accounts of Louverture's reading when he was a younger man – 'a black Spartacus, the negro Raynal predicted would avenge the outrages done to his race'. Louverture in return shouted to the crowd gathered at the Place d'Armes on that April day, 'After God, Laveaux!'[54]

The trust placed in Louverture by the French government seemed to be fully warranted – as Louverture had put it in a letter to the French Republican government in early 1797: 'We will not delay in making the English feel the brunt of a courage born of liberty.'[55] Yet off the battlefield, Louverture was increasingly showing an additional skill for effectively sidelining a number of rival political figures in Saint-Domingue. After putting down attempts to overthrow Laveaux's authority, Louverture suggested Laveaux himself leave Saint-Domingue to become the colony's elected representative in the French National Convention in order to counter the growing pro-slavery lobby in Paris which had accompanied the fall of Robespierre and the rise of the Directory.[56] Laveaux acquiesced, leaving in October 1796, and in May 1797 Louverture was appointed the new General in Chief of the Republican army in Saint-Domingue by the new French commission. Louverture declared his apparent supreme confidence that the British, for all their reputation, resources and prestige, could be beaten. As he wrote optimistically to Laveaux on 23 May 1797, 'I can only believe that with the help of God we shall soon purge the French territory of the tyrannical hordes who have infested the colony for too long, and that soon we shall form a single, unified family of friends and brothers'. The preservation of Saint-Domingue, Louverture repeated, is 'assured' while France 'can count upon my irrevocable zeal as its true defender'.[57]

The French were certainly in no position to question Louverture's 'zeal'. Though on occasion the British had managed to defeat Louverture on the battlefield, when their cavalry were able to cut his army down in open country, Louverture was a proven master of guerrilla warfare and rapid troop movement and the occasions his forces came off worse were rare.[58] Korngold notes that while the longest march ever attributed to Napoleon Bonaparte across mountains in a single day was 52 kilometres, 'Toussaint marched his army sixty-four kilometres in a single day through mountainous territory with only a trail to guide him'.[59] Evidence of the skill of Louverture's troops at not only guerrilla warfare but also conventional warfare (when not facing cavalry in open country) can be seen from Howard's account of their storming and ultimately capturing several forts around Saint Marc in early June 1797 while the main British detachment was away, trying to dislodge Louverture's forces at Mirebalais. By 1 June 1797, after its first terrible year in Saint-Domingue, Howard's original contingent of York Hussars had already been reduced from almost 700 men to just 234 men of all ranks, and now they faced another battering.[60] On 3 June 1797, Howard notes 'a very formidable Column with Cannon made its Appearance before the Gros Morne & began to prepare to attack it . . . the Column that advanced against the Gros Morne came on to the Assua[l]t with the utmost Intrepidity . . .'. On 4 June, 'they stormed Gros Morne three different times & at the last carried it by superiority of Numbers . . . the Next Morning the Enemy began to fire from an eighteen . . . [pounder] & a Howitzer on Camp Gilliam . . .'.[61]

The 6th, in the Morning, a twenty four Pounder and Howitzer was opened against Fort Churchill, which battered to Breach [the wall] all that Day . . . the Enemy having Possession of Camp Gilliam immediately pushed on their advances towards the Town & the Next Morn: began to play on the Town from a Battery they had erected on an Eminence that immediately overlooked it. About ten OClock on the Morning of the Seventh [of June] the four and

twenty . . . [pounder] having made a Breach in the Walls of Fort
Churchill large enough to attempt an Assault, The Enemy came-on
in three Columns of about 1500 Men each, with a determination
to take the Fort – if Possible . . . [62]

Though ultimately this counter-attack by Louverture's forces failed
to take Saint Marc, Dubois notes the bravery of the black troops at
Fort Charvill as they 'found their ladders were too short to scale the
walls, and tried to take the fort by standing on one another's shoulders
at the top of the ladders, while "their dead piled up around them"'.[63]

In early 1798, one British officer, Captain Marcus Rainsford,
witnessed a review of several thousand of Louverture's troops while
passing as an American sailor in Cap Français after his ship ran into
a hurricane and he was forced ashore. Rainsford's recollections also
testify to Louverture's training of his soldiers in not just guerrilla
warfare and discipline but also mass attack:

Each general officer had a demi-brigade [regiment], which went
through the normal exercises with a degree of expertness I had
seldom before witnessed. They performed, excellently well,
several manoeuvres applicable to their method of fighting. At a
whistle a whole brigade ran three or four hundred yards, and then,
separating, threw themselves flat on the ground, changing to their
backs and sides, and all the time keeping up a strong fire; after
this they formed in an instant again into their wonted regularity.
This single manoeuvre is executed with such facility and precision,
as totally prevents cavalry from charging them in bushy or hilly
country. Indeed, such complete subordination prevailed – such
promptitude and dexterity, as must astonish any European soldier
who had the smallest idea of their previous situation.[64]

Off the battlefield itself, Louverture also taught the British other
lessons in the conduct of warfare, as can be seen from his correspondence with British Brigadier-General John Whyte, the aptly named
defender of white supremacy who was one of the commanders of
the British military occupation of Saint-Domingue. Louverture had
written to Whyte to reassure him that he need not worry about the

British prisoners of war captured by his black Republican forces, as he had arranged for them to go to Port-au-Prince. 'The fortunes of war have delivered into my hands a number of British officers, among whom is Major Hally. The mutual consideration civilised men owe one another and the dictates of humanity, have prompted me to take all necessary measures to insure their entire safety.' However, when Louverture found an order on one captured free coloured auxiliary officer fighting for the British, Lepointe, stating 'No quarter for the brigands! Take no prisoners!', Louverture wrote again to Whyte:

> You have demeaned yourself in the eyes of this and future generations in allowing one of your commanders (the cowardly Lepointe) to issue this order, which could not have been issued without your knowledge . . . And that in spite of the fact that I have given instructions to my commanders to treat all prisoners with humanity.
>
> I am only a black man. I have not had the advantage of the fine education the officers of His Britannic Majesty are said to receive; but were I to be guilty of so infamous an act, I should feel I had sullied the honour of my country.[65]

Before too long, black troops serving under the British began to see that the British position was hopeless and began to defect to Louverture's forces. The British occupation was proving hugely costly to the British state in terms of both blood (about 12,500 men out of 20,500 in total sent to Saint-Domingue would die, with almost another 1,500 sent home injured) and of treasure (something like a cost to the British state of £5,765,000 all told, not including military pay to rank and file, plus equipping and transporting the troops, which would take the total over £7 million for the five years 1793–98).[66] With roughly three out of five British soldiers who were sent to Saint-Domingue dying there, there was a growing call back in Britain for the troops to come home, with Edmund Burke among those attacking the disastrous campaign. 'In these adventures, it is not an enemy we had to vanquish but a cemetery to conquer . . . Every advantage is but a new demand on England for recruits to the West Indian grave.'[67] In March 1798, the young general Thomas Maitland

– who, as we have seen, had long been doubtful about the British occupation of Saint-Domingue – replaced Brigadier-General Whyte to take command of the British army there, with the orders to oversee British withdrawal. Maitland now negotiated with Louverture directly, first to relinquish Saint Marc and Port-au-Prince, and then finally Jérémie in the South and Môle in the North.[68] As Michael Duffy has judged, the 'bloody defeats' which led to 'the British withdrawal from Saint-Domingue' in 1798 'terminated the attempt to establish a major new Empire in the West Indies', and the Americas more generally, on the part of the British.[69]

The Seizure of State Power

As well as overseeing the British exit, Louverture also successfully masterminded what Michel-Rolph Trouillot called 'the conquest of the state machinery', forcing out potential internal challengers to black power in Saint-Domingue, beginning with Sonthonax.[70] Having cleared his name in France, the generally popular and sincere abolitionist Sonthonax had returned to the colony as part of a new French commission in May 1796, alongside the free coloured activist Julien Raimond and Philippe Rose Roume de Saint-Laurent. However, Sonthonax soon clashed with Louverture over a number of issues, including that of the place of returning white former slave-owning émigrés in Saint-Domingue. After Louverture welcomed the return of his former master Bayon de Libertat in July 1797, Sonthonax had reminded him of the law on émigrés, 'condemning those who have aided or favoured their return to four years in irons'. In August 1797, Louverture responded to this thinly-veiled threat with one of his own, a letter similar to the one he had previously sent to Laveaux, though this time signed by other leading black generals including Moïse and Christophe, suggesting it was best Sonthonax return to France to champion the cause of the colony in France. Within a few days Sonthonax had taken the hint and was on a ship back to Paris.[71]

The French Directory responded by sending General Joseph d'Hédouville, who arrived in May 1798, to enforce a tougher line than that of Sonthonax and Raimond in order to limit Louverture's growing power, as well as that of the emerging new ruling class of black officers. In addition to trying (and failing) to lure Louverture to leave Saint-Domingue with him for France, and being humiliated by the independent diplomacy Louverture had demonstrated with respect to negotiating the British exit, Hédouville attempted to develop a more independent civil service bureaucracy that would be loyal to him and metropolitan France, as a counterbalance to Louverture and the military. The inevitable tensions all this manoeuvring provoked reached a climax when Hédouville tried to replace Moïse as commander of the Fifth Regiment with Manigat, a black magistrate. This sparked not only a violent confrontation with Moïse himself, but also a wider rising backed by Louverture, culminating in a march on Cap Français by Dessalines's Fourth Regiment with their orders to arrest Hédouville.

Faced with this insurrection by the black officer class of Saint-Domingue, Hédouville wisely chose in October 1798 to leave Saint-Domingue for France with his supporters, including the retired delegate to the French National Convention, Belley. He had lasted six months.[72] As he departed, Hédouville divested the limited powers left at his disposal with the only other figure on Saint-Domingue with anything like an independent power-base that might counter that of Louverture, the free coloured general André Rigaud.[73] But as Louverture now boasted in a speech revealing of his new confidence,

> Hédouville says that I am against liberty, that I want to surrender to the English, that I wish to make myself independent; who ought to love liberty more, Toussaint Louverture, slave of Bréda, or General Hédouville, former Marquis and Chevalier de Saint-Louis? If I wished to surrender to the English, would I have chased them away? . . . Remember that there is only one Toussaint Louverture in San Domingo and that at his name everybody must tremble.[74]

Louverture certainly had reasons to feel so self-confident, for over the course of the past five years he had gone from an obscure black leader with a few hundred troops under him, armed mainly with lances and machetes, to effectively controlling, by 1798, the local state machinery on Saint-Domingue. He now commanded 'a devoted army of veterans, numbering at least 13,000 to 14,000, as against Rigaud's 8,000', and these troops were now additionally armed with rifles.[75] Louverture had overseen the defeat of the Spanish and now the British, and also the extension of emancipation to the whole colony of Saint-Domingue for the first time – as Dubois notes, 'a major diplomatic and military triumph'. Louverture wrote to Laveaux triumphantly in September 1798, 'I found, my dear general and good friend, the colony dismembered, ruined, sacked, occupied by the rebels, the émigrés, the Spanish and the English' when he had joined the French Republican forces back in 1794. Now, 'I am leaving it peaceful, purged of its external enemies, pacified, and advancing towards its restoration'.[76] As Laveaux put it, paying tribute to Louverture's achievement in Paris,

> It is to the brave general Toussaint Louverture that the republic owes this precious advantage; he mounted a general attack with such wisdom and organization that the frightened English had to surrender in order to retreat; already they have left our lands. Such is the work of this general who is faithful to his oaths, who is tightly tied to the French republic . . . I remember with pleasure that already in the year 5 [1797] . . . I tried to describe him to you. I told you, citizen representatives, '*they dare to call him a disorganiser!*'[77]

If Louverture had grown in confidence, just as striking was the growth in self-assurance of the army he had built around him. For British reactionaries like Edmund Burke, the blacks of Saint-Domingue were of course barely worth consideration, given that they were simply a 'race of fierce barbarians'.[78] In fact, as C.L.R. James put it, by 1798 and the expulsion of the British from the island, the Haitian Revolution 'had created a new race of men'.

> This change had first expressed itself in August 1791 . . . but they were soon formed into regiments and were hardened by fighting. They organised themselves into armed sections and into popular bodies . . . At bottom the popular movement had acquired an immense self-confidence. The former slaves had defeated white colonists, Spaniards and British, and now they were free. They were aware of French politics, for it concerned them deeply. Black

men who had been slaves were deputies in the French Parliament, black men who had been slaves negotiated with French and foreign governments. Black men who had been slaves filled the highest position in the colony. There was Toussaint, the former slave, incredibly grand and powerful and incomparably the greatest man in San Domingo. There was no need to be ashamed of being a black. The revolution had awakened them, had given them the possibility of achievement, confidence and pride. That psychological weakness, that feeling of inferiority with which the imperialists poison colonial peoples everywhere, these were gone.[79]

Louverture's 'Black Jacobinism'

In *The Black Jacobins*, James rightly situated the Haitian Revolution within the wider age of bourgeois-democratic revolutions, and showed how Louverture's extraordinary career rose in conjunction with the radicalisation of the revolutionary process unfolding in France after 1792.

> The great [French] revolution had propelled him out of his humble joys and obscure destiny, and the trumpets of its heroic period rang ever in his ears. In him, born a slave and the leader of slaves, the concrete realization of liberty, equality and fraternity was the womb of ideas and springs of power, which overflowed their narrow environment and embraced the whole of the world.[80]

Presenting Louverture as not only the quintessential 'black Jacobin', but also a French General, this chapter has examined how, after joining the French Republican forces in 1794, Louverture now inspired and led the black insurgents to stunning victories over first Spanish and then British imperial armies over the next four years. The ideals of the Enlightenment, of liberty, equality and fraternity, now more than ever became a material force to be reckoned with in Saint-Domingue, embodied in the black rebel army. For James, during this mighty collective struggle for freedom, long-held and cherished beliefs in kingship among the former enslaved were steadily transcended. Louverture, who understood that the revolutionary slogans of liberty and equality were 'great weapons in an age of slaves', 'used them with a fencer's finesse and skill', and was central to ensuring it was the new ideas which triumphed over the old.[81]

We have seen how Louverture clearly championed 'black Jacobinism' in his ideological engagements with Jean-François and Dieudonné, but it is worth examining also how the ideals of *The Declaration of the Rights of Man and the Citizen* in 1789 and the National Convention's abolition decree of 16 Pluviôse an II in 1794 equally fired his rhetoric when addressing his own fighters. On 18 May 1797, in an 'Address to soldiers for the universal destruction of slavery', published in the *Bulletin officiel de St-Domingue*, Louverture declared:

> Let the sacred flame of liberty that we have won lead all our acts ... Let us go forth to plant the tree of liberty, breaking the chains of our brothers still held captive under the shameful yoke of slavery. Let us bring them under the compass of our rights, the imprescriptible and inalienable rights of free men. [Let us overcome] the barriers that separate nations, and unite the human species into a single brotherhood. We seek only to bring to men the liberty that [God] has given them, and that other men have taken from them only be transgressing His immutable will.[82]

In 1796, Louverture had even sent his two sons to be educated in revolutionary France, writing to Laveaux in May 1797 that 'I send into your care my beloved children, whom I miss dearly. May God look over their days and bestow upon them His grace, that they may profit from the education that France grants them, to render themselves one day worthy of expressing their gratitude!'[83] However, perhaps the high watermark of Louverture's republicanism and rhetorical 'black Jacobinism' came in his 'Letters to the French Directory' in October and November 1797, which defended the principle of universal human rights against those – including those in and around the increasingly conservative Directory itself, such as Vincent Marie Viénot de Vaublanc, a notable champion of the slave-owners of Saint-Domingue in the new National Assembly – who were considering the case for the return to slavery across the French Empire. In October 1797, Louverture had challenged the hypocritical logic of Vaublanc for daring to try and claim some kind of moral high ground over the Haitian revolutionaries while defending Atlantic slavery and the slave trade:

> If, because some blacks have committed some cruelties, it can be deduced that all blacks are cruel, then it would be right to accuse of barbarity the European French and the nations of the world . . . citizen Vaublanc pours all the odium merited by actions so criminal as to be equally reproved by the laws of nature and the social order; but why, at the same time, doesn't he apply himself to tarnishing the monsters who have taught these crimes to the blacks and who have all been, by a barbarous guild on the coast of Africa, wrenching the son from his mother, the brother from his sister, the father from his son . . . outrages committed in cold blood by civilized men like himself who were therefore more atrocious since they committed evil knowingly, allowing the lure of gold to suppress the cry of their conscience . . . Will the crimes of powerful men always be glorified?[84]

As for the threat to re-impose slavery in the French Empire, Louverture wrote in November 1797, 'The attacks the colonists propose against this liberty must be feared all the more insofar as they hide their detestable projects under the veil of patriotism':

> Could men who have once enjoyed the benefits of liberty look on calmly while it is taken from them! They bore their chains when they knew no condition of life better than that of slavery. But today when they have left it, if they had a thousand lives, they would sacrifice them all rather than to be subjected again to slavery. But no, the hand that has broken our chains will not subject us to them again. France will not renounce her principles. She shall not permit the perversion of her sublime morality and the destruction of the principles that honour her the most, and the degradation of her most beautiful accomplishment, by rescinding the decree of 16 Pluviôse that honours so well all of humanity. But if, in order to re-establish servitude in St-Domingue this were to be done, I declare to you that this would be to attempt the impossible. We

have known how to confront danger to obtain our liberty, and we will know how to confront death to preserve it.[85]

As James eloquently wrote – in words with which it is worth concluding – though Louverture was a 'soldier and administrator' who had once experienced the barbarism of slavery, his declaration

Figure 1　Portrait of Toussaint Louverture by Pint van der Benjamin (ca 1798). Photograph of watercolour original in the Steel Maitland collection (GD193/7/5), National Records of Scotland. Reproduced courtesy of Messrs Dickson Middleton, Chartered Accountants.

in this 1797 letter is 'a masterpiece of prose excelled by no other writer of the revolution'.

Leader of a backward and ignorant mass, he was yet in the forefront of the great historical movement of his time. The blacks were taking their part in the destruction of European feudalism begun by the French Revolution, and liberty and equality, the slogans of the revolution, meant far more to them than to any Frenchman. That was why in the hour of danger Toussaint, uninstructed as he was, could find the language and accent of Diderot, Rousseau, and Raynal, of Mirabeau, Robespierre, and Danton. And in one respect he excelled them all. For even these masters of the spoken and written word, owing to the class complications of their society, too often had to pause, to hesitate, to qualify. Toussaint could defend the freedom of the blacks without reservation, and this gave to his declaration a strength and singlemindedness rare in the great documents of the time.[86]

4

The Black Robespierre:
1798–1801

In late 1798, after despatching Hédouville, Louverture dined with his adopted nephew General Hyacinthe Moïse. In his mid-20s, Moïse was already one of Louverture's most trusted and able lieutenants, and no doubt seen as a potential future leader. As C.L.R. James noted, over dinner, Louverture 'expressed himself fully . . . one of the few occasions on which we get a glimpse into his mind'.

> Hédouville has spread it that he is going to France to seek forces to come back . . . I do not want to fight with France, I have saved this country for her up to the present, but if she comes to attack me, I shall defend myself. General Hédouville does not know that at [*sic*] Jamaica there are in the mountains blacks who have forced the English to make treaties with them? Well, I am black like them, I know how to make war, and besides I have advantages that they didn't have; for I can count on assistance and protection.[1]

Taking inspiration from the maroon communities in the Blue Mountains of Jamaica, who had won autonomy from the British colonial authorities through war during the 1730s, Louverture, as we have noted, also began to undertake independent negotiations with the English in the figure of General Thomas Maitland to facilitate withdrawal of British forces – something that officially should have been overseen by a representative of France. Indeed, alongside figures like Laveaux in Paris, who made a fine speech in 1798 celebrating the fourth anniversary of the abolition of slavery on the 16 Pluviôse an II, the British were now among those Louverture thought he could begin to count on for 'assistance and protection' against any potential French counter-revolutionary intervention.[2] When Louverture met Maitland at the Môle in late August 1798, he was gifted a 'sumptuous meal' and presented with 'the splendid silver that had decorated the table' from the king of England.[3] Louverture hoped that the British might help him rebuild the colony's economy after seven years of revolutionary warfare, through trade with British merchants which would both give him another source of potential provisions and goods the colony needed, and give him a new market to which to export coffee and sugar. Louverture therefore took the opportunity now to sign a secret treaty with the British that ended their economic blockade of the island in return for his promise not to spread his revolution to the nearby British slave colony of Jamaica. The treaty did not remain particularly 'secret' for long, and on 12 December 1798, the *London Gazette* announced: 'With this treaty, the independence of this important island has, in fact, been recognised and guaranteed against any efforts the French might make to recover it.'[4]

The British and French were still at war at this point, and so there was little the French authorities in Paris could do immediately as Louverture began in practice to play one imperialist power off against another, and to exercise the kind of political and economic autonomy from metropolitan France the previous colonial master planter class on the island had always wanted to exercise. France's new representative in colonial Saint-Domingue after Hédouville, the commissioner Philippe Roume, supposedly overseeing Louverture, had been reduced to playing a largely ceremonial role in Cap Français. Emboldened by the weakness of the Directory in Paris, Louverture now sought to restart trade with America, which had been suspended in June 1798 after repeated attacks on American merchant shipping by French privateers. After Louverture had made personal approaches to the American President John Adams and promised to welcome US ships as those of an ally and protect them from attack, in early 1799 the US Congress passed an act allowing the president to reopen bilateral trade. Louverture now negotiated a trade agreement with US consul general Edward Stevens, which allowed him to source guns and ammunition from North American merchants, and soon the ports of Saint-Domingue were heaving with American and British merchant shipping.[5]

Yet just as the price paid for the relative security and autonomy of maroon communities in Jamaica was their willingness to betray and help put down revolts by the enslaved on the island, so Louverture now showed he was also willing to fulfil the terms of his agreement with the slave-owning British Empire. Isaac Sasportas, a young merchant from a family of Sephardic Jews who was inspired by the ideals of the French Revolution, had convinced Roume to begin preparing a 4,000-strong invasion force to seize Jamaica, and then he himself secretly slipped into the British slave colony in late 1799 to try to help lay the ground by planning to poison the governor's coffee on Christmas Day 1799 in the hope of sparking an indigenous uprising. Louverture secretly informed the British colonial authorities of Sasportas's plans to export revolution in order to maintain commercial and diplomatic links with Britain and the United States, and Sasportas and his co-conspirator were arrested, imprisoned and hanged in Kingston, two days before Christmas.[6]

The Fall of Rigaud

As a powerful figure who had long established his military reputation and was now emerging as a statesman and diplomat, Louverture had established a daringly independent foreign policy – for instance, making trade and non-aggression treaties with Britain and America in 1798–99 for the good of colonial Saint-Domingue instead of loyally championing metropolitan France – and this had long sent alarm bells ringing in Paris. Within Saint-Domingue, there was only one figure who had anything like a comparable power base to match Louverture – André Rigaud – and now the French government did their best to inspire the free coloured leader to use his independent army which occupied the south to bring down Louverture. As we have noted, before being expelled from the colony, Hédouville had placed his trust in Rigaud, and in a private letter to him denounced the 'perfidy of General Toussaint Louverture, who is sold to the English, the émigrés, and the Americans'. Hédouville urged Rigaud to challenge Louverture, noting further: 'I absolve you entirely of the authority he was given as general-in-chief.'[7] Back in Paris, Hédouville's report to the Directory spelt out the thinking behind the French plan of 'divide and rule':

The export of sugar and coffee by English and American boats will make money flow in the colony, and [Louverture] will not fail to attribute this state of things to the wisdom of his government. I am no less convinced that sooner or later this precious island will escape from French domination. I do not take it on myself to propose the measure you will take to weaken the power of those who dominate it, but if the moment is not yet ripe for taking vigorous measures, it will perhaps appear to you important to create germs of division between them, to embitter the hate that exists between the Mulattoes and the blacks, and to oppose Rigaud to Toussaint.[8]

As C.L.R. James notes, following Hédouville's departure, Louverture now saw it was a strategic necessity to exert his authority in the South, for 'the great danger now was a French expedition and it was suicidal to allow Rigaud and his Mulattoes to remain in control of the South and West'. This is where the French were likely to land, as Rigaud 'would most certainly welcome a French force and ensure the ruin of the black state'.[9] Louverture initially hoped it might be possible to win over the other critical charismatic free coloured leader Louis-Jacques Bauvois to his side, and so marginalise Rigaud and take control of the South without the need to wage any major war. However, Beauvois was torn between loyalty to Louverture and to Rigaud, and so refused to throw his support behind one or other figure – which may have been decisive – and played little part in the looming so-called 'War of the South' or 'War of the Knives', as it was later known.[10] Though it was a war waged for territorial control, inevitably it became increasingly coloured by a racial dynamic as old resentments between black and free coloured came to the fore when the fighting began.[11] Both Louverture and Rigaud accused each other of rebelling against legitimate French authority, with Rigaud alleging that under Louverture the colony 'was to be sold to the British government, and once more brought under the Yoke of

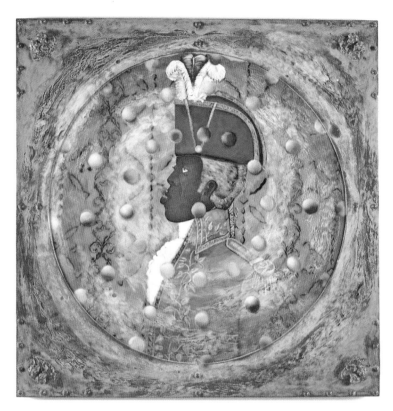

1.   Edouard Duval-Carrié – 'Le Général Toussaint Enfumé' (General Toussaint Wreathed in Smoke, or Pretty in Pink), 2003 © the artist

2. François Cauvin – 'Toussaint L'Ouverture', 2009 © the artist

3. Ulrick Jean-Pierre – 'Cécile Fatiman' © the artist

4. Lubaina Himid – 'Scenes from the life of Toussaint L'Ouverture, 5', 1987 –
Arts Council Collection, Southbank Centre, London © the artist

The text below the illustrations reads:

'Toussaint's wife lived on a plantation in
the interior, and devoted herself to the
cultivation of coffee. Whenever Toussaint
could escape from his duties he went there.'

'Did she help him with strategy?'

5.   Kimathi Donkor – 'Charles and Sanité Belair', 2004 © the artist

6. Charlot Lucien – 'Caché à l'histoire: Toussaint Louverture enfermé au Fort de Joux' (Hidden from history: Toussaint Louverture imprisoned at the Fort de Joux)

7.   Haitian mural of Jean-Jacques Dessalines (1991), from Pablo Butcher, *Urban Vodou: Politics and Popular Street Art in Haiti* (Signal Books, 2010). Courtesy of Pablo Butcher.

8.   Haitian mural paying homage to Toussaint Louverture (1986), from Pablo Butcher, *Urban Vodou: Politics and Popular Street Art in Haiti* (Signal Books, 2010). Courtesy of Pablo Butcher.

Slavery' – to which Louverture alleged that it was the free coloureds fighting under Rigaud who had dreams of restoring slavery for the black masses.[12]

The audacious Rigaud struck first in June 1799, taking Petit-Goâve from Louverture's officer Laplume, by way of revenge for Laplume's previous role in weakening Rigaud's authority when he had undermined Dieudonné a few years earlier. Alexandre Pétion, an important free coloured officer with a renowned elite cavalry force, now defected from Louverture to join Rigaud, and would soon find himself valiantly holding Jacmel under siege from Dessalines. Louverture himself was forced to venture north to put down revolts around the Môle and Port-de-Paix. As Dubois notes:

Louverture had enemies everywhere. Indeed, he was the target of two assassination attempts. In the first, his personal physician was killed, and a bullet passed through Louverture's hat. During the second Louverture's carriage was riddled with bullets and his coachman killed. The general escaped 'miraculously' only because he was riding behind the carriage. It was the greatest political challenge Louverture had yet faced.[13]

However, a combination of calculated brutal repression of these new risings in the North and West, a blockade by the US Navy of southern ports on Louverture's request, and sheer superior numbers under arms eventually saw Louverture regain the initiative in this increasingly bloody war. Rigaud also found it hard to rely on support from cultivators in the South under his control given his harsh labour regime, and placed his hopes on support from France – support that never came. Dessalines on the other hand came into his own in the battle against Rigaud's forces in the South, waging what Nick Nesbitt has called 'a total war of utter brutality'.[14]

In November 1799, the coup of 18 Brumaire brought Napoleon Bonaparte to power as First Consul in France, ending the rule of the Directory. As Korngold notes, 'at the commencement of his political career Napoleon asked his advisors what colonial system had given the best financial results. He was told that that it was the system prevailing before the Revolution. "Then," said the former Jacobin, "the sooner we return to it the better."[15] On 25 December 1799, Bonaparte wrote a letter to the citizens of Saint-Domingue outlining his new constitution, Article 91 of which stated that French colonies will be ruled by 'special laws'. This overturned the Directory's commitment to governing colony and metropole under the same law and constitution, as reiterated in its 1798 'Law on the Colonies'.

Indeed, Bonaparte's 'special laws' hinted so strongly at a return to the *ancien régime* system – and even a restoration of the highly profitable system of colonial slavery – that he felt the need to write a special letter pleading that 'the Consuls of the Republic, in announcing to you the new social pact, declare to you that the SACRED principles of the freedom and equality of blacks will NEVER SUFFER among you the least attack or modification'.[16] Bonaparte was still at war with Britain and so he was playing for time, and amidst his proclamations conceded that Louverture was still the 'general-in-chief' of the army of Saint-Domingue. When Bonaparte's emissary landed in Saint-Domingue with news of these proclamations confirming Louverture's authority in June 1800, they therefore represented a major blow to Rigaud. In late July 1800, Rigaud and his family fled the colony, eventually making their way to France – leaving Louverture to consolidate his control over the whole of Saint-Domingue, and now in conditions of relative peace for the first time.[17] Victory in the brutal war from 1799–1800 ensured Louverture's hegemony and his position as unquestionably the dominating political figure in Saint-Domingue. As he would soon put it, 'if Bonaparte is the first man in France, Toussaint is the first man in the Archipelago of the Antilles'.[18]

Liberty Against the Law

Amidst the bloody civil war in the South, as Dessalines's troops confronted Rigaud's forces, those among the formerly enslaved who were still trapped working on the plantations mostly looked on nonplussed at the two rival armies. As a Vodou song that seems to have been coined in this period put it, 'Mister Rigaud, Mister Dessalines, this land is not for us. Understand? It's for the whites'.[19] Louverture had over the past few years opened up colonial Saint-Domingue to returning white émigrés from the United States and elsewhere, as he believed they were necessary to reconstruct the colony's plantation economy, something essential if colonial Saint-Domingue was to keep metropolitan France happy enough for them not to even think of reneging on their stated commitment to the cause of anti-slavery. Louverture would soon invite white wealthy former planters like Barnard Borgella, the former mayor of Port-au-Prince, to help advise him on policies. However, on returning to their estates, émigré planters often found it increasingly hard if not impossible to reclaim their land and what was left of their houses from the formerly enslaved, who since emancipation had grown increasingly confident and aspired to forge new lives of freedom by cultivating small plots of land as independent farmers amidst the ruins of old plantations.[20] Ever since issuing their emancipation proclamations of 1793, Sonthonax and Polverel had tried to confront this new 'problem of freedom' by trying to force those amongst the formerly enslaved who were not needed as soldiers back to work on the plantations. As Polverel had put it bluntly to cultivators in 1794: 'This land does not belong to you. It belongs to those who have bought it or inherited it from those who first acquired it.'[21]

> You can lay claim to the products of this land only through agriculture. And I have told you that the portion assigned to you in the revenues of the land will be given to you *only in compensation for your work* . . . Before, you had no share in the profits of the plantations. Today each of you will have his share in these profits, in proportion to his work.[22]

Polverel also enshrined gender inequality into the new pay and conditions of wage slavery, something that the women black cultivators had tried to overturn, and he tried to justify this along the following lines when addressing male cultivators.

> Finally, your women grumble about the inequality of my proposed system of shares because I have allotted them less than the men. Why give us less than the men, they say? Don't we all go to work at the same time? they ask. Don't we all quit at the same time? . . .

They want us to ignore the natural inequality in the strength of men and women, their usual or regular ailments, and the periods of rest they need for pregnancies, childbirth, and nursing . . . Africans, if you want these women to be reasonable, be reasonable yourself.[23]

Such words were backed up with new laws, and those who resisted this new system of domination on the plantations were punished with fines, prison or forced labour on public works. While some ran away to form maroon communities as in the days of slavery in Saint-Domingue, and while some men took their chances as soldiers, the remaining workforce of men and women were left to face the brave new world of exploitation and oppression as best they could.[24] The reports sent to Polverel by managers of the plantations testified, however, to plenty of examples of continuing resistance, as for example the note written by Lacolle, the manager of the Codère plantation in the south, on 20 March 1794:

I am sending you two African women who refused to work at night after the decision of the plantation's administrative council. Not only did they refuse to work, but they also said the worst things to the *commandeur*, threatening him and saying that he would be the one working in the sugar mill at night. I therefore ask you to punish them as an example.[25]

In those areas that his forces helped liberate from the Spanish and the British, Louverture's approach was very much in keeping with the pattern laid down by Sonthonax and Polverel. Indeed, Louverture invested in plantations of his own. As Louverture emphasised in a proclamation on 22 March 1795, private property was to be respected. 'Work is necessary,' he stated, 'it is a virtue. It is the general good of the state. Every lazy and errant man will be arrested to be punished by the law. But service is also conditional and will be paid a just wage.'[26] However, small-scale revolts on the plantations continued sporadically, and in June 1795, in Marmelade, a rising took place which left several plantation managers dead after cultivators denounced Louverture for 'making them work' in order to return them to the 'slavery of the whites'. Louverture recalled heading straight there in his customary manner 'to preach' at the rebellious labourers, but 'in thanks for my pains I received a bullet in the leg, which is still causing me a great deal of pain'.[27]

In February 1796, plantation workers in the northwestern mountains near Port-de-Paix, producing coffee for sale to American traders in return for food and munitions, had revolted in response to the dismissal of Etienne Datty, a local black *commandeur*. Louverture rode overnight to negotiate with the rebels and 'preach' at them his take on freedom under the universal rights based law offered by the French Republic. As he wrote to Étienne Laveaux on 20 February 1796, on arriving in Port-de-Paix he took register of the local mood of the 'large number of farmers, both men and women, [who] came to me with food, some chickens and eggs'. 'They told me how glad they were to see me and that they hoped I would put an end to these disorders. I ordered them to get me hay, which they did immediately and seemed to do with pleasure. I took this to be a good sign that it would not be difficult to resolve things.'[28]

When confronted by Étienne Datty and 500 rebellious labourers, many of whom were armed, Louverture calmly told them to form a circle.

> I mounted my horse and entered the circle where, after having condemned the murders they had committed, I told them that if they wished to preserve their liberty they would have to submit to the laws of the Republic, and be docile and work, that it was only in this way that they would benefit from their freedom.[29]

This 'freedom' had little to offer to the rebellious formerly enslaved black workers, who pointed out that the new *commandeurs* who had replaced Datty were bullying managers:

> We are looked down upon, they vex us at every turn. They don't pay us what we are owed for the food we grow. They force us to give away our chickens and pigs for nothing when we go to sell them in the city, and if we complain, they have us arrested by the police, and then make us pay to get out. You see, general, that one is not free if he is treated like this.[30]

Louverture had little answer to this, except to ask in reply how he could assure the National Convention back in Paris that blacks were 'fit to be free' and would not just 'no longer work, and . . . steal and kill' if they were now liberated, with this kind of attitude? Louverture stressed that 'it was up to them to prove that they wanted peace and tranquillity by all of them returning immediately to their respective plantations and starting back to work, and that this was entirely up to them', but if they did so they would be pardoned, a course of action which was accepted.[31]

On 25 April 1796, the new paternalist and elitist logic of Louverture's argument – a far cry from his earlier attacks on Sonthonax for trying to 'impose' freedom from above – was more explicitly put when addressing his 'brothers in the commune of Saint Louis du Nord', when he called them 'my wayward children' who were 'shunning the advice of a father who adores them': 'You are free; what more can you want? What will the French people who are ready to arrive here say when they learn that, having been given this gift, you have been so ungrateful as to dip your hands in the blood of their children?'[32]

Like Sonthonax, Louverture now glorified the French Republic, who had apparently 'given this gift' of freedom, even though the French Revolution itself was now spiralling down into counter-revolution, and power in Paris was now in the hands of the conservative Directory:

But, brothers and friends, I know you are, by yourselves, incapable of these atrocities. Crime-laden monsters who no longer dare show themselves have been seeking to lead you with them into the abyss . . . They have led you astray by telling you that France will return you to slavery! How could you believe such an atrocious slander? Don't you know how much France has sacrificed for universal liberty and the rights of man? Young people of dazzling ability, the most flourishing commerce, the greatest treasures of Europe, the most formidable navy, palaces without number, the richest industries: that is what France has sacrificed for universal freedom and human happiness! . . . No, citizens, this generous and magnanimous people has too noble a soul to ever plan such a project.[33]

Louverture's welcoming of returning former émigrés was in part about working to rebuild towns and schools, and develop a new anti-racist culture on Saint-Domingue – and there were clear registers of success here, with for example some of the grand theatres re-established in Cap Français with black actors taking centre stage. As James notes, 'race prejudice, the curse of San Domingo for two hundred years, was vanishing fast', not least because of the 'stigma of colour could not flourish' when so many blacks and people of colour held high posts in government.[34]

One British officer visiting Saint-Domingue from his base in Jamaica just before the British occupation ended, Marcus Rainsford, recorded how he 'immediately perceived that the usual subordinations of society were entirely disregarded, and that he was to witness, for the first time, a real system of equality.' Visiting a coffee house, Rainsford records that:

Here were officer and privates, the colonel and drummer, at the same table indiscriminately . . . Toussaint not unfrequently dined here himself, but he did not sit at the head of the table, from the idea, (as was asserted,) that the hours of refection and relaxation should not be damped by the affected forms of the old regimen, and that no man should assume a real superiority in any place than the field . . . the men were in general sensible and polite, often dignified and impressive, the women frequently elegant and engaging. The intercourse of the sexes was on the most rational footing, and the different degrees of colour which remained had lost most of that natural hostility that formerly existed . . . the situation of those . . . who formed the great bulk of the people, was indeed very greatly changed.[35]

Yet if white visitors and returning émigrés were impressed by what they saw as a new 'system of equality' emerging, the experience of the black majority was somewhat different. In November 1798, after the British departure from Saint-Domingue, Louverture had issued a proclamation requiring all able-bodied blacks in the colony no longer needed by the army be forced to return to work for wages on the plantations.[36] This greatly pleased the white émigrés, as did the fact that in January 1800 Louverture – officially a Catholic – became the first of many black leaders in Saint-Domingue to try and stamp out Vodou, outlawing 'nocturnal assemblies and dances', even though (and again like many future black heads of state in the island) he himself might have personally continued to secretly practice the religion.[37]

The contradictions of Louverture's class position, presiding over a policy of conscription with respect to plantation labour, are also apparent in his 12 October 1800 'Proclamation on Labour'. This forced labour decree stressed again that work was critical 'to ensure freedom', as 'agriculture supports governments, because it promotes commerce, comfort and abundance, gives birth to the arts and industry, and keeps all occupied'. If only 'every member of society works, the result is public tranquillity; troubles disappear along with idleness, which is the mother of vice, and each enjoys in peace the fruits of his labours . . .' However, Louverture bemoaned the fact that, 'since the revolution, farmers, both men and women, who, since they were young at the time, were not engaged in farming, do not wish today to take part in it because, they say, they are free, and so spend their days running about aimlessly, thus setting a very bad example for the other farmers, while all the while generals, officers, their subordinates, and soldiers are engaged in permanent activity to protect the sacred rights of all . . .'[38] This went to the nub of the question of 'freedom', that amidst conditions of almost permanent war for several years, followed by a bloody civil war, colonial Saint-Domingue was marked by the growth of a bloated militaristic state superstructure. The society rested moreover on an economic base of increasingly bitter and exploited cultivators apparently destined to spend most of their lives working on plantations under bullying managers with little way out in sight. No wonder many workers resisted Louverture's rural code of laws in whatever ways they could, from a form of 'go-slow strikes' on the plantations to outright absenteeism which would allow them to spend at least some time on their own kitchen gardens.[39]

If a strong economy was essential to support a large standing military force, which was itself required to ensure adequate defence against the clear and ever-present danger of external intervention,

Louverture's army was also used internally, through a network of army officers functioning as district inspectors with authority over plantation work, to force cultivators to keep working on plantations when they wished to found smallholdings of their own. The unpopularity of this militarisation of plantation labour – together with Louverture's encouragement of white plantation owners to return to and reinvest in their former estates – led to increasing resistance among black labourers, many of them women, who found all previous possible routes of escape from the plantation increasingly blocked. Old white planters grew in confidence, daring to announce to their former chattel slaves turned wage slaves that: 'You say you are free! But you are going to be forced to come back onto my property, and there I will treat you as I did in the past, and you will see that you are not free.'[40] The struggle for what Christopher Hill in a different context once called 'liberty against the law' intensified in 1801, as Louverture introduced a new decree effectively outlawing cultivators to form local small settlements by pooling resources to buy a small plot of uncultivated land to work away from the discipline of the plantations. If an available plot was smaller than about three acres in size, it was now not allowed to be sold, so keeping the prospect of land-ownership out of reach for most rural workers, while if such a plot was larger it had to be approved and monitored by local administrations under Louverture's control. As Dubois notes, 'the decree made it impossible for relatively poor men and women to acquire land. There were to be only wealthy landowners and landless workers, with nothing in between.'[41] Carolyn Fick notes that Louverture was 'forging a society with no real foundation', while 'the one sector of Saint Domingue society in which Toussaint would have found his most logical and most natural ally, the mass of black labourers, stood in fundamental opposition to his own social and economic philosophy'.[42]

Louverture's Constitution

In January 1801, Louverture sent 10,000 troops led by Moïse into neighbouring Santo Domingo – then officially French territory, having been ceded by Spain in 1795, but still largely controlled by

Spanish administrators – in order to deprive any future invading French army of use of Santo Domingo's harbours.[43] Moïse's forces met little resistance, and in less than a month Louverture at last found himself in control of the whole island of Hispaniola, having defied explicit instructions from France by placing Santo Domingo under formal military occupation. To consolidate his position and power base, Louverture imprisoned Philippe Roume for refusing to approve the invasion and occupation of Santo Domingo. On 4 February 1801, Louverture now convened an assembly – which included free coloured figures such as Julien Raimond, an emissary of Bonaparte, and Bernard Borgella, the white planter and mayor of Port-au-Prince, but tellingly not a single former enslaved African aside from himself – to draft a new constitution for colonial Saint-Domingue. This was a strategic response on the part of Louverture to Bonaparte's recent stress on 'special laws' for the colonies through a bid for greater autonomy, and also a way of consolidating his own unchallenged position of power. 'I have taken flight into the realm of the eagles, and I must be prudent as I descend to earth. I can no longer be placed but on a rock, and this rock must be the constitutional cornerstone that will guarantee my power for as long as I shall live.'[44]

The assembly completed its work in May 1801 and the new constitution was promulgated in June and July of 1801. As Nick Nesbitt notes, it represented:

the first modern constitution to address the conflict between the defence of property rights and human rights: if all humans possess a fundamental and inalienable freedom, property rights must logically be explicitly qualified not to include humans. Aside from Robespierre's never-adapted 1793 proposal for just such a constitutional limitation, this constitution was the first in Western modernity explicitly to base itself on the unlimited, universal right to freedom from enslavement.[45]

So although Article 13 declared that '[p]roperty is sacred and inviolable', this was overruled by Article 3 which declared '[t]here cannot exist slaves on this territory, servitude is therein forever abolished. All men are born, live and die free and French.'[46] The gendered bias notwithstanding, there was a meritocratic strand to the constitution, with Article 4 declaring that '[a]ll men, regardless of colour, are eligible for all employment'.[47] However, Article 14 reinforced the forced nature of work on the plantations, noting 'the colony being essentially agricultural cannot suffer the least disruption in the works of its cultivation'.[48] In many ways, the constitution was rather regressive, paternalistic and authoritarian – representing a retreat even from the ideals espoused in metropolitan France. In terms of religion, therefore, Article 6 reinforced the earlier ban on Vodou, and stressed that '[t]he Catholic, apostolic, Roman faith shall be the only publicly professed faith', a shift from the Radical Enlightenment in its proscriptive reactionary attack on religious pluralism in favour of Catholicism.[49] Accordingly the constitution declared for marriage, and against divorce.[50]

More critically, Louverture's constitution of 1801 could not be described as democratic, for it concentrated power in the hands of one autocratic figure, 'the Governor'. Article 19 declared that '[t]he colonial regime is determined by laws proposed by the Governor and rendered by a gathering of inhabitants, who shall meet at fixed periods at the central seat of the colony under the title Central Assembly of St-Domingue'.[51] The initial Central Assembly of Saint-Domingue was to be nominated by the Governor in the first instance, but this would be subject to renewal every two years where a more elective element would be introduced into proceedings. The Central Assembly would meet in secret and 'vote the adoption or the rejection of laws that are proposed to it by its Governor'. The constitution revealed that the Governor in the first instance was to be Louverture himself, who because of his 'steadfastness, activity, indefatigable zeal and rare virtues' was to be entrusted with the position 'for the remainder of his glorious life', with the right to nominate his successor in case of his death, after which the post would be renewed at five-year terms.[52] To reinforce the autocratic nature of the new regime, Article 67 noted that 'there cannot exist in the colony corporations or associations that are contrary to public order. No citizen association shall constitute a civil association [*société populaire*]. All seditious gatherings shall be dissolved immediately, first by way of verbal order and, if necessary, by armed force'.[53]

However, significantly, this new constitutional arrangement made no explicit reference to the ultimate authority of metropolitan France in colonial Saint-Domingue, aside from Article 27 which noted the Governor 'corresponds directly with the government of the Metropole, on all matters relative to the interests of the colony'.[54] While the constitution ruled out formal independence from the French Empire, it was suggestive of self-determination, self-government and autonomy, and a new sister-republic status in a 'commonwealth' structure.[55] As Louverture declared when he promulgated it, 'Forever live the French Republic *and* the colonial constitution'.[56] This was a path-breaking step forward, and an explicit challenge to the idea of 'special laws' for the colonies. Louverture sent the constitution to Bonaparte via a French officer, Charles Humbert Marie Vincent, with a letter written on 16 July 1801, in which Louverture optimistically noted how 'this constitution was received by all classes of citizens with transports of joy that will not fail to be reproduced when it is sent back bearing the sanction of the government'.[57]

The Moïse Uprising

That Louverture could declare that his new constitution 'was received by all classes of citizens with transports of joy' in Saint-Domingue seems to reveal something of his own growing detachment from the great mass of the people. Though the length of the working day on the plantations had now been limited, and use of the whip was prohibited, Louverture's generally draconian labour laws, together with his overtures to the feelings of white émigrés, who had been central to drafting the new constitution, led to bitter resentment and frustration among not only black labourers, but also sections of the new black ruling class of officers. As Roume noted in September 1801, 'a furious storm is gathering against him . . . the first officer of known merit who will put himself at the head of the malcontent will get the entire colony to rise in less than two weeks'.[58] While figures like Dessalines and Christophe were loyal enough to Louverture to implement repression when needed against the former enslaved black workers as part of the forced militarisation of agriculture, others like Moïse found it an affront to the spirit of the revolution to do so. As

Moïse, general of the Northern Province in 1801, put it, he could not 'resolve himself' to be the 'executioner of my colour', not least when he was being asked to do so on behalf of what he saw as white French metropolitan interests. 'I will love the whites only when they have given me back the eye they took from me in battle', Moïse declared. He was happy instead to defy his uncle's decrees prohibiting the selling off of small plots of land to soldiers and officers. Moïse had led the invasion of Santo Domingo in early 1801, ostensibly to stop the Spanish participation in the trans-Atlantic slave trade, and so he was now very disturbed by Louverture's recent decision – revealed in the 1801 constitution – to support the potential re-introduction of the slave trade to Saint-Domingue, in order to guarantee a supply of labour for the great plantation estates.[59] Louverture's refusal to push for independence from France and expel the French was also seen by Moïse as something of a betrayal of the revolution, and he had once told his secretary that 'if it were in my power, I would soon be rid of them' as 'you have to finish what you start'.[60]

In late October 1801, a series of labour rebellions ultimately encompassing some 6,000 farm workers rocked the region under Moïse's control, the Northern Province, and several hundred whites were killed – including Bayon de Libertat, Louverture's friend and former master. The cry of the rebels had been 'Forward Moïse!' and 'General Moïse is with us – death to all the whites!'[61] While Dessalines bloodily set about restoring 'law and order' in what were once the revolutionary cockpits of August 1791 (parishes such as Dondon, Marmelade, Plaisance, and Limbé), Louverture accused Moïse (the local district inspector) of being the 'soul and leader' of the rebellion, and eventually executed him by firing squad without trial. Another veteran officer whose revolutionary credentials went back to August 1791, Joseph Flaville, was also executed, alongside many other rebels.[62] On 25 November 1801, a clearly shaken Louverture issued a new 'Proclamation', declaring that although agriculture was 'the most honourable, and the most useful of all occupations', for many of the cultivators on the plantations, 'since the revolution, perverse men have told them that freedom is the right to remain idle and follow only their whims. Such a doctrine could not help but be accepted by evil men, thieves and assassins. It is time to hit out at the hardened men who persist in such ideas.'[63] It was not just men in Louverture's sights, as his social conservatism now came to the fore, attacking in his proclamation 'the horde of vagabonds and women of ill repute' in the cities.[64] The execution of Moïse underlined Louverture's willingness to discipline the new black ruling class through terror if necessary, in order that they accept his authority and his strategy for rebuilding the plantation economy, even if it meant fatally weakening his own organic ties to the great mass of plantation workers. 'Idleness is the source of all disorders, and if it is at all tolerated, I shall hold the military commanders responsible, persuaded that those who tolerate idleness and vagabonds are secret enemies of the government.'[65]

That someone previously so loyal as Moïse could – in Louverture's eyes at least – betray him, suggested his authority was less secure than he had previously thought. Louverture recalled how he had had in depth conversations with Moïse 'for ten years', and how in

a thousand of my letters . . . at every opportunity, I sought to explain to him the holy maxims of our faith . . . instead of listening to the advice of a father, and obeying the orders of a leader devoted to the well-being of the colony, he wanted only to be ruled by his passions and follow his fatal inclinations: he has met with a wretched end . . .[66]

Amidst what Dubois calls his 'delirium', Louverture now drew up 'a charter for a new police state'.[67]

Any individual, man or woman, whatever his or her colour, who shall be convicted of having pronounced serious statements tending to incite sedition shall be brought before a court martial and punished in conformity with the law. Any Creole individual, man or woman, convicted of making statements tending to alter public tranquillity but who shall not be worthy of death shall be sent to the fields to work with a chain on one foot for six months. Any foreign individual found in the case of the preceding article shall be deported from the colony.[68]

Louverture imposed a system of surveillance and policing of mobility through compulsory identity cards for all men and women in municipal administrations to be bought, signed by the mayor and local police superintendent, and renewed every six months.

> It is expressly ordered that municipal administrators are only to deliver security cards to persons having a known profession or state, irreproachable conduct and well-assured means of existence. All those who cannot fulfil the conditions rigorously necessary to obtain a security card will be sent to the fields if they are Creole, or sent away from the colony if they are foreigners.[69]

If Nick Nesbitt is right to call the forcible militarisation of agriculture a 'totalitarian social model', then the November 1801 proclamation underlines how Louverture was increasingly constructing a totalitarian style regime with punitive forms of chain gang labour to enforce that model.[70]

The Black Robespierre

In Louverture's defence, it needs of course to be recognised that his tough measures and state capitalist economic programme managed to achieve what Dubois calls 'a remarkable revival of the shattered plantation economy in Saint-Domingue'.

> By 1801, according to official reports, coffee exports had risen from almost nothing to two-thirds of their level in 1789. Improvements in the sugar industry, where damages were more difficult to repair, were smaller, and included little of the more profitable refined sugar, but by 1802 exports were at one-third of those of 1789. These official figures did not include a significant amount of underground and contraband trade . . . under Louverture's control, the rebuilding of many sectors of Saint-Domingue's plantation economy was well under way.[71]

Moreover, as Victor Kiernan once noted, Louverture was 'not only a fighter of genius', but 'a statesman with a vision of his island as a fatherland, a new nation'.

Such an idea could have come to him from his French books; but this was a land of divided races, white and brown and black, and he was almost alone in thinking of a country in which they could all join hands, instead of a domination of one over the others ... it was an experiment far ahead of its time, one that various multi-racial countries are trying today ... [In Saint-Domingue], after ages of atrocious oppression and years of bloodshed, it may have been an impossible one.[72]

However, that Louverture had been forced to establish a harshly repressive military dictatorship reveals his essential failure to defend the new liberty of a post-emancipation society through the forced militarisation of plantation labour. As Frederick Engels had once noted with respect to the revolutionary early sixteenth-century German peasant leader Thomas Müntzer, 'the worst thing that can befall a leader of an extreme party is to be compelled to take over a government in an epoch when the movement is not yet ripe for the domination of the class which he represents, and for the realisation of the measures which that domination implies'.

What he *can* do depends not upon his will but upon the degree of contradiction between the various classes, and upon the level of development of the material means of existence, of the conditions of production and commerce upon which class contradictions always repose. What he *ought* to do, what his party demands of him, again depends not upon him or the stage of development of the class struggle and its conditions. He is bound to the doctrines and demands hitherto propounded ... thus, he necessarily finds himself in an insolvable dilemma. What he *can* do contradicts all his previous actions, principles and immediate interests of his party, and what he *ought* to do cannot be done. In a word, he is compelled to represent not his party or his class, but the class for whose domination the movement is then ripe ... whoever is put into this awkward position is irrevocably lost.[73]

Louverture was forced in effect to begin to act in the interests not of the black cultivators or ordinary insurgent soldiers of

Saint-Domingue, but in the interests of a nascent, emerging ruling land-holding black class of army officers, becoming steadily more aloof and detached in the process.[74] Louverture's crushing of the 'Moïse revolt' in 1801 merely underlined his failure to solve 'the problem of freedom' by rebuilding the colony's prosperity through forced, military style plantation labour. However, the manner in which Louverture became 'irrevocably lost' was not through any personal corruption of power; nor was he, like Napoleon Bonaparte, 'destroyed' by his 'own ambition', as David Geggus has charged.[75] Rather, like the Jacobin Maximilien Robespierre, the 'black Jacobin' Toussaint Louverture was quite 'incorruptible' in that sense, and if anything his 'ambition' did not go far enough, for rather than prepare the people of Saint-Domingue for a fight for full independence from metropolitan France he always strived to work within the system for colonial autonomy within the French Empire.

Indeed, as C.L.R. James noted, the fall of Louverture is comparable to that of Robespierre himself, who as a bourgeois revolutionary had ultimately turned the Terror from the aristocrats onto the *sans culottes* and their leaders in 1794. As James put it, Robespierre 'destroyed his own left-wing and thereby sealed his own doom' in Thermidor, when 'right-wing and left in the Convention combined to strike at this sinister dictator, and when he sent out the call to the people he could not get the old response'.[76] Similarly, for James, although Louverture was not so strictly a 'bourgeois revolutionary' in the classic manner of a figure like the lawyer Robespierre, nonetheless 'to shoot Moïse, the black, for the sake of the whites was more than an error, it was a crime. It was almost as if Lenin had had Trotsky shot for taking the side of the proletariat against the bourgeoisie . . .'. James continues:

> Toussaint crushed the revolt as he was bound to do. But instead of recognizing the origin of the revolt as springing from the fear of the same enemy that he was arming against, he was sterner with the revolutionaries than he had been before. Instead of reprisals Toussaint should have covered the country, and in the homely way that he understood so well, mobilised the masses, talked to the people, explained the situation to them and told them what he wanted them to do. As it was, the policy he persisted in reduced

the masses to a state of stupor . . . Toussaint, like Robespierre, destroyed his own Left-wing, and with it sealed his own doom . . . He ignored the black labourers, bewildered them at the very moment that he needed them most, and to bewilder the masses is to strike the deadliest of all blows at the revolution.[77]

If the 'Moïse revolt' had underlined the extent to which Louverture's new constitution in 1801 had not been 'received by all classes of citizens with transports of joy' in colonial Saint-Domingue, in Paris Bonaparte, who had now made himself Consul for life, would not exactly be moved to 'transports of joy' on reading it either. Bonaparte had previously been unable to make up his mind about Louverture and Saint-Domingue, but hearing of both the invasion of Santo Domingo and the new constitution drove him into fury.[78] As Carolyn Fick notes, 'coming from a former slave who had reached the summit of power and dared, as a black and as an equal, to confront the First Consul, the constitution struck a direct blow at the ontological foundations of white supremacy and, by its very existence, at the colonial foundations of the Atlantic colonial order'.[79] As James notes, when Vincent presented Louverture's constitution, 'Bonaparte swore at Vincent, cursed the "gilded Africans", said that he would not leave an epaulette on the shoulders of a single nigger in the colony . . . Bonaparte called Toussaint a "revolted slave", called Vincent a coward and drove him from his presence'.[80]

More critically, with France's war with Britain drawing towards a temporary close, and with the preliminary peace negotiations which would culminate in the Treaty of Amiens already underway, Bonaparte now saw an opportunity to finally settle accounts with this 'revolted slave' and re-impose metropolitan authority through his own 'special laws' in colonial Saint-Domingue, and with them the restoration of slavery. The British, for all their earlier apparent admiration for the heroic Louverture while they were at war with France, were now happy to give Bonaparte the green light for any invasion.[81] As the British Government put it to the governor of Jamaica, 'Toussaint's black empire is one amongst many evils that have grown out of the war – and it is by no means our interest to prevent its annihilation.'[82]

For all the ways in which Louverture's new system of domination on the plantations had come to resemble the barbaric bondage of slavery, the formerly enslaved of Saint-Domingue nevertheless knew themselves that there was a crucial difference between the past and the present, one for which they had already given their lives in their thousands to establish and defend, and one for which they would be prepared if necessary to do so again. Sonthonax in his time had distributed 20,000 muskets to black field-hands, using proclamations in Kreyòl explaining that this was so they could defend their new freedoms themselves.[83] Louverture, following in Sonthonax's footsteps, and seeing the gathering storm clouds ahead, had in the past bought 30,000 muskets from America and stressed in numerous speeches to the black labourers, while brandishing and pointing to a musket: 'This is your liberty!'[84] Now the storm was about to break.

5

The Harder They Come, The Harder They Fall . . . : 1801–03

By the late 1790s, as we have seen in the previous chapter, the return of Saint-Domingue to relative stability following the upheavals in the middle of that decade allowed Toussaint Louverture to introduce a series of policies aimed effectively at allowing reconstruction of the plantation economy. The formerly enslaved were transformed into *cultivateurs*, but their freedom nevertheless remained heavily policed. Growing confidence over the success of Louverture's approach as well as the progressive extension of his power base had led to the publication of his constitution in 1801. Slowly distancing himself from the people for whose interests he had fought throughout the previous decade, Louverture also found himself the subject of Bonaparte's wrath. The constitution named the Haitian leader governor-for-life, and the First Consul interpreted this increase in his rival's political authority as a direct personal attack. C.L.R. James sees in Louverture's manoeuvres direct anticipation of Bonaparte's own plans for the colony: 'Toussaint was perfectly right in his suspicions. What is the regime under which the colonies had most prospered, asked Bonaparte, and on being told the *ancien régime* he decided to restore it, slavery and Mulatto discrimination.'[1] The Haitian constitution was then primarily more a reactive and anticipatory statement enshrining the principle of individual liberty than the commitment to independence that would emerge forcefully following Louverture's imminent departure from the colony. The text can be read in particular as a response to Bonaparte's own constitution of 1799, which had implied a refusal to grant colonial subjects the equal rights of French citizens and seemed to anticipate an eventual return to slavery throughout the empire.

By the time Louverture's envoy Vincent had arrived in Paris to present the constitution to Bonaparte, it is likely that plans to wrest back power from the Haitian revolutionaries were already in motion. Despite the failure of his campaign in Egypt, Bonaparte was consolidating his power both nationally and internationally, meaning that the possibility of continued resistance in the colonies, and in particular the spread of the revolutionary movement beyond Saint-Domingue, would have been seen as a threat. As Europe returned temporarily to peace (the Treaty of Amiens would finally be signed in March 1802, with a preliminary agreement having been agreed the previous September), a portion of the French army was now available for a transatlantic mission to defeat Louverture and re-establish the former colonial order in Saint-Domingue. There has been much speculation about the detailed motivations behind this move, with some seeing Bonaparte responding to the lobbying of planters seeking to recover their lands and possessions, others blaming his wife Joséphine, herself from a family of Martinican planters, for influencing his decision.[2] Although he undoubtedly received advice and pressure from multiple sources, neither of these explanations seems to hold water. It is most likely that Bonaparte's decision to resort to force in Saint-Domingue was part of a larger strategy to reassert power over the only parts of the *ancien régime* empire with which France still maintained clear links, as well as to exploit the Louisiana territory acquired from Spain in 1800 in a wider attempt to reassert the colonial (and economic) authority over North America diminished following the Seven Years War in 1763.

After several months of prevarication, Bonaparte began to plan the expeditionary force. This would be – as James notes – 'the largest expedition that had ever sailed from France, consisting of 20,000 veteran troops, under some of Bonaparte's ablest officers'.[3] The ambitious scale of the undertaking was in direct proportion to the First Consul's steadfast decision, apparent from October 1801 following the delivery of the Saint-Domingue constitution by Vincent, to remove Louverture from power altogether. Preparations were both military and diplomatic, for Bonaparte also had to ensure safe passage of his fleet through negotiations with Britain and the USA, both of which were understandably suspicious of the implications of the French plans for the balance of power in the region. Bonaparte also sought – and failed to secure – clear support from the USA for the provision of the staples and ammunition the French forces would require. In terms of the military planning, the troops initially selected for the expedition had already proved themselves in conflicts in a variety of contexts, including France itself, where some of those recruited had suppressed counter-revolutionaries in guerrilla warfare in the Vendée. Less battle-tested soldiers would only be deployed when, some months into the campaign, the staggering high losses – victims of the resistance of the opposition as well as the tropical climate – had become apparent. The officers deployed initially were equally experienced, not least because a number were eager for further action unavailable in a Europe returned to peacetime. Pamphile de Lacroix – the French general and author who left a comprehensive account of the campaign – claims that the force 'was composed of an infinite number of soldiers with great talent, good strategists, great tacticians, officers of engineers and artillery, well educated and very resourceful'.[4] In a last minute change of leadership, Bonaparte put his brother-in-law and political ally General Charles Victor-Emmanuel Leclerc in command, a decision often seen as an indication of the importance of the expedition as well as of his desire to retain close control. The two men had served together in the Italy campaign, and although Leclerc was inexperienced (almost entirely so when it came to colonial matters), he could at least be trusted, which was of paramount importance given the impossibility of micromanaging the expedition from the other side of the Atlantic. The General, initially reluctant to take on the role, was accompanied by his wife, the First-Consul's sister Pauline, who insisted on bringing with her artists, musicians and other courtiers. As James mordantly notes: 'Slavery would be re-established, civilization restarted, and a good time would be had by all.'[5]

The expedition – including several of Louverture's political opponents, not least Rigaud and Pétion, but also Louverture's sons Isaac and Placide, who had been at school in France and were now being returned by Bonaparte to Saint-Domingue – left Brest in early

December 1801, following delays caused by bad weather. Further ships left Cherbourg, Le Havre and Toulon the following month, meaning that their arrival in the Caribbean would be staggered. The degree of preparation for the specifics of the challenge in Saint-Domingue was, in a number of respects, limited. Girard reports that Leclerc, '[m]istaking the hilly, forested terrain making up much of Saint-Domingue's interior for the sand dunes of Egypt, asked that a regiment of dromedary riders be sent with the expedition'.[6] Bonaparte also failed to heed any of the lessons learnt by the British during their disastrous campaign in 1793–98. As a result of problems with procurement, rations transported were limited, meaning that the expedition would be obliged to supplement these on the ground; and Bonaparte's assumption that Louverture would be defeated swiftly in the winter left his army vulnerable to the tropical diseases they would have to handle should – as would be the case – that goal not be achieved.

Like Louverture himself, Bonaparte understood the potential tactical benefits of keeping his intentions to himself. His plan was reliant on deception as much as on military force. Leclerc carried with him a number of letters from his superior, one of which – stressing the pacific intentions of the expedition – was entrusted to Isaac and Placide. The First Consul had sought initially to reassure the population of Saint-Domingue regarding his plans, which he claimed would respect the abolition of slavery in 1794. In a decree of 8 November 1801, he had implied, however, that it was Louverture (as opposed to himself) who now constituted a threat to their freedom:

> Whatever your origin or your colour, you are all French, you are all free and all equal in the sight of God and of the Republic . . . The government is sending you Captain-General Leclerc. He is bringing with him a large force to protect you against your enemies and the enemies of the Republic. If people tell you: 'These troops are intended to take away your freedom', you should reply, 'The Republic will never allow it to be taken from you.'[7]

Leclerc had clear instructions to break black military power and to restore white privilege, but he had no explicit authority to restore slavery, in part to avoid such incendiary information falling into the wrong hands. His challenge was to avoid any impression that his troops had been sent to overturn the achievements of the Revolution, a task that from the outset would prove impossible, not least because, when his forces after over six weeks at sea sighted Saint-Domingue in late January 1802, Leclerc was hasty to invade the colony and assert his authority. He expected, as Girard reports, 'all the negroes to lay down their arms when they see an army'.[8] His inexperience and ignorance of warfare in the Caribbean would rapidly become apparent.

Louverture had already been made aware by French newspaper reports of the departure of Leclerc's fleet. Still shaken by reactions to his execution of Moïse, he travelled around the country preparing for an assault. It is claimed that he rushed back from Santo Domingo to witness the arrival of the expedition, and exclaimed on seeing it: 'We are going to die. The whole of France has come to Saint-Domingue. She comes to avenge herself and force the blacks back into slavery.'[9] Louverture reached Cap Français as swiftly as he could to support Henri Christophe, who was in command of the town. On 2 February 1802, Leclerc had already sailed into the harbour with a section of his troops. Christophe prepared to receive him, not surprisingly since both armies still in principle served the same republican cause; but on Louverture's orders, he managed to hold him at bay for two days. As soon as he understood the intentions of French, Christophe eventually ordered the second destruction of Cap Français, which, once the population had withdrawn to the hills, was razed to the ground. Leclerc had expected to land in a prosperous city, but was instead greeted with smouldering ruins. The challenges of the forthcoming campaign were immediately apparent. Riding from Cap Français to Gonaïves, Louverture met a group of French troops led by General Jean Hardy, and was nearly killed when they opened fire on him. Hostilities had broken out in earnest, meaning that both sides were forced to seek a strategy to deal with the situation – marked for the French by difficult terrain and a hostile environment, for the Haitian revolutionaries by increasing uncertainty over their loyalties – in which they found themselves.

Leclerc sought to launch a propaganda offensive, seeking further to undermine claims and rumours that he had been sent to re-establish slavery. He welcomed those among the generals of Saint-Domingue who wished to join his side, leaving Louverture in an increasingly ambiguous and indeed weak position with many of his former allies now refusing to rally to his cause. 'War is a continuation of politics by other means,' noted C.L.R. James, 'and Toussaint was now reaping the reward of his policy during the previous year. The labourers, hostile to the French, did not respond to his call. They could not understand why Toussaint should call on them to fight these whites, when all his policy had been towards conciliation of them.'[10] Leclerc actively took advantage of this confusion, taking by force the town of Léogane and the city of Port-au-Prince (which had been renamed Port-Républicain in 1793 by Polverel). The newly arrived General Rochambeau also took Fort Dauphin (later known as Fort-Liberté). The collapse of Louverture's vision for Saint-Domingue was apparent, and he responded by planning a campaign of violent resistance. In a letter to Dessalines on 8 February 1802, written therefore just after the landing of Leclerc four days earlier, he outlined a calculated commitment to a continuation of the Revolution through a campaign of guerrilla warfare against an imperial army that sought not only to overturn the gains of the 1790s but also to re-impose slavery. In the hostile welcome granted to the French expedition, Henri Christophe had already initiated this response by razing the town. We see in Louverture's orders an unconditional commitment to defending general emancipation:

Do not forget, while waiting for the rainy season which will rid us of our foes, that we have no other resource than destruction and flames. Bear in mind that the soil bathed with our sweat must not furnish our enemies with the smallest aliment. Tear up the roads with shot; throw corpses and horses into all the fountains; burn and annihilate everything, in order that those who have come to reduce us to slavery may have before their eyes the image of that hell they deserve.[11]

C.L.R. James nevertheless detects here a tactical flaw, considering this approach to have been adopted too late, allowing Leclerc to make inroads into the colony: 'His desire to avoid destruction was the very thing that caused it. It is the recurring error of moderates when face to face with the revolutionary struggle.'[12] Dessalines, despite never receiving the letter, continued to pursue Leclerc's forces doggedly as Louverture's key ally, finding weak points where they were depleted, and burning to the ground towns he knew he could not hold.

Louverture himself remained guarded about his tactics. His troops sang French revolutionary songs, seeking to suggest that they – as opposed to Leclerc's forces – were the true guardians of the values of the French Revolution. Mindful of his strategic disadvantage and despite the violent resistance he orchestrated, he still hoped to negotiate with Leclerc. The French general exploited this possibility by deploying Isaac and Placide Louverture in the way Bonaparte had imagined he should when he included them in the expedition. The boys were sent, together with their tutor Coisnon, to Louverture's plantation at Ennery, where they presented their father with the letter sent by Bonaparte, in which the First Consul denied any intention to restore slavery and asking him to support Leclerc in governing the country. The meeting was by all accounts an emotional one, and has been the subject of a number of subsequent dramatic representations (most notably in the work of Lamartine). Louverture was indignant that his sons were being used as political pawns, in an attempt to engineer his surrender. It became clear that the choice he was being offered was a false one: either submit to Leclerc as his first lieutenant, or refuse loyalty and be declared an outlaw. Louverture understood where submitting to an invading army containing a number of his enemies such as Pétion and Rigaud would lead, noting that 'in the midst of so many disasters and acts of violence I must not forget that I wear a sword.'[13] He rejected Coisnon's offer, but gave his sons the choice as to which side they would join. Isaac sided with France, although his mother persuaded him to stay with her; Placide stood by his father, and was immediately placed in command of a battalion of Louverture's guards. 'His family,' notes Girard, 'like his colony, was torn in half.'[14]

Leclerc's offer had in part been a ruse, an attempt to play for time as he waited for reinforcements. When these arrived, on 17 January 1802, his campaign to regain control of the colony began in earnest. Louverture was declared an outlaw, and the French generals sought, in a pincer movement, to surround what was left of his army and neutralise it. With half of his 18,000 troops having defected to the French, the revolutionary leader's options were limited, and he resorted to a guerrilla approach that led Leclerc to declare to Bonaparte: 'We are fighting an Arab-style war here.'[15] Women joined the resistance, as had been the case in the earlier years of the Revolution, operating as fighters and also as sources of intelligence given the relative freedom of movement they were allowed. Sanité Belair, born in 1781, who had married an officer and later general in Louverture's army, Charles Belair, in 1796, rose, for example to become a lieutenant in her own right in Louverture's army.[16] Fighting reached high levels of intensity in the region between the West and North provinces, culminating in two memorable battles in the Ravine-à-Couleuvre and at Crête-à-Pierrot, the second of which still plays a particularly important role in Haitian memory.

C.L.R. James describes in detail the unfolding of this first stage of the War of Independence, and stresses the extent to which troops on both sides were the product of the revolutionary struggles of the past decade, with the French soldiers drawing their strength, skill and resolve from their contribution to the destruction of feudalism and a series of struggles for the values of 1789 across Europe. James underlines again, however, the extent to which the Haitian revolutionaries were pushing to a logical extreme, in ways perhaps unimaginable to the French, the values of liberty and equality: 'the few thousand who remained faithful to Toussaint were the advance-guard of the revolutionary army fighting a revolutionary war [. . .] the liberty and equality which these blacks acclaimed as they went into battle meant far more to them than the same words in the mouths of the French. And in a revolutionary struggle these things are worth many regiments.'[17] James notes how in time the French army 'went to pieces' and 'some soldiers deserted to the blacks', including the famous case when 'a regiment of Poles, remembering their own struggle for nationalism, refused to join in the massacre of 600 blacks, ordered by Leclerc, and later, when Dessalines was reorganising the local army, he would call one of his regiments the Polish regiment'.[18]

Fought on 23 February 1802, Ravine-à-Couleuvre ('Snake Gully') was the type of battle that Louverture had sought actively to avoid as

Figure 2 Karl Girardet & Jean Jacques Outhwaite, 'Saint Domingo, from the Ravine-à-Couleuvres ["Snake Gully"]'. Courtesy of the Napoleon Collection, Rare Books and Special Collections, McGill University Library.

it was a more conventional engagement than the guerrilla campaigns he was seeking to wage. With only 600 troops and several hundred additional armed *cultivateurs* dispersed in the woods to impede the progress of the French forces, Louverture attacked Rochambeau and his soldiers as they passed through the steep-sided valley. The combat was brutal, and the Haitian leader – insistent on leading his troops – was nearly killed, but the significant deaths among the French were proof that his strategy was having an effect. Whereas some of his officers, most notably Dessalines, needed little encouragement to pursue an implicit policy of total war, against not just the French expeditionary forces but also whites in the colony more generally, others continued to shift their allegiance to Leclerc. Christophe, Dessalines and Louverture nevertheless exploited their experience of military struggle over the past decade, and managed to maintain the networks of communication on which their resistance depended.

The culmination of this stage of the conflict occurred at Crête-à-Pierrot, a strategically located hill fort in the Cahos mountains on the valley of the Arbonite river, originally abandoned in the initial struggles with Leclerc's forces, but which Louverture requested that Dessalines should subsequently seek to hold. The battle lasted from 4–24 March 1802. Besieged by 2,000 of Leclerc's troops, Dessalines put up a strong defence, causing 400 French fatalities. The French attacked the fort again a week later, but were repelled once again with significant casualties, leading Leclerc to return with artillery and additional troops. Faced by Leclerc's determination to take the position and preparing to abandon the fort, Dessalines made a rousing speech in which, for the first time and in striking contrast to Louverture's own pronouncements, he invoked independence:

They will start off strongly, but soon they'll be slowed down by illness, and will die like flies. Hear what I say: if Dessalines surrenders to them a hundred times, he will betray them a hundred times . . . we'll harass them, we'll fight them, we'll burn their harvests, then we'll hide in our hills where they can't get us. They won't be able to hold the country, and they'll have to leave it. Then I'll make you independent. We don't need whites among us anymore.[19]

On 24 March, Dessalines again abandoned the fort at night as a result of the heavy losses he was suffering, and the French regained control of it. Their victory was, however, a pyrrhic one, for Leclerc suffered major losses, including several of his more senior officers. 2,000 French troops in total had been killed taking a fort defended by only 1,200 rebels, a fact that Leclerc took major efforts to disguise. For Louverture, the propaganda value of the siege was immense, in particular in that it demoralised French troops who struggled to understand why their enemies were singing the revolutionary songs they knew themselves, and also allowed the formerly enslaved to see that their struggle could inflict major, even disproportionate harm on the invading forces. As C.L.R. James notes, 'To read English and French accounts of their operations in San Domingo one would believe that but for yellow fever they would have been easily victorious', but the strength of resistance among Louverture's remaining forces and their commitment to the ideals of the Revolution also created significant disruption to Leclerc's plans. The revolutionary leader attempted to exploit this situation by triggering spontaneous rebellions against the French among the *cultivateurs*, but running into the troops of Maurepas on his way to Port-de-Paix, he realised as they began to fire on him that his former general had also defected to Leclerc. On paper, despite Louverture's tactical advantage and intimate knowledge of the territory, the French now had military superiority, especially as the reinforcements had arrived. The effectiveness of guerrilla manoeuvres became came increasingly unclear as more of Louverture's generals began to join Leclerc. With diminishing numbers of supporters, the revolutionary leader was reduced to an increasingly isolated position. Eventually, by the beginning of May, Christophe, who had initially razed Cap Français at Leclerc's approach, had surrendered to the French general and joined his forces. It is likely that neither of them knew that Louverture had been also preparing since early April for his own surrender, on condition that Leclerc be returned to France.

This point in the campaign coincides with Bonaparte's decision at last to signal publicly his intention to overturn any French commitment to antislavery. Making the slave trade legal in the French empire, he was careful to announce that slavery would persist in those colonies where technically it had never been abolished, although he tactically failed to make any mention of Saint-Domingue or Guadeloupe. When this news reached the latter island, violent resistance broke out, led by Colonel Louis Delgrès. French troops under the command of Antoine Richepance cornered Delgrès in Fort Saint Charles, in what became known as the battle of Matouba. On 28 May 1802, Delgrès and his followers died in an act of self-immolation rather than accepting the re-imposition of slavery, igniting their own ammunition stores. The links between Delgrès and Louverture are striking, evident not least in their uncompromising commitment to the defense of universal emancipation. In April 1998, plaques to the memory of both men were placed in the French Pantheón, outside the cell to which the remains of the French abolitionists Abbé Grégoire and Victor Schoelcher had been transferred. There is also a striking parallel between Louverture and the rise and fall of General Thomas-Alexandre Dumas – father of the famous novelist Alexandre

Dumas – who was born in Saint-Domingue of mixed heritage and rose to a division general in the French revolutionary armies, the highest-ranking person of African descent ever in a European army. As C.L.R. James noted, the French revolution had appointed 'that brave and brilliant Mulatto, General Dumas, Commander-in-Chief of one of its armies, but Bonaparte detested him for his colour, and persecuted him'.[20]

In revolutionary Saint-Domingue, the spread of details of Bonaparte's counterrevolutionary intentions was more closely policed, although there is clear evidence of his plans in diplomatic correspondence, where coded references to the re-imposition of slavery allude to an 'agricultural plan'. Given the numerous reassurances he had provided regarding the maintenance of the freedom of the formerly enslaved, Leclerc would later make it clear in a letter to the Minister of the Navy in August 1802 that he considered it the responsibility of his successor and not himself to re-establish slavery:

> I think I will be able to do everything so that the person who replaces me will have nothing to do but put into effect the government order, but after the innumerable proclamations I have issued here assuring the blacks of their freedom, I do not want to have to contradict myself. Assure the First Consul, however, that my successor will find everything in place.[21]

It was in this context of subterfuge and double-speak that Leclerc used Christophe as an intermediary to treat with Louverture. The Haitian revolutionary leader agreed to surrender in return for several conditions: freedom would be respected for all on the island; all officers of his army would be integrated into the French forces and be allowed to maintain their rank; and Louverture himself could retire to a location of his choice in the colony, retaining his staff. Louverture and Leclerc at last met in person on 7 May 1802, at Cap Français, but the Haitian leader refused the French general's overtures, including the offer of the post of lieutenant-general, and also rejected offers to dine: according to James, such was his fear of poisoning that 'near the end of the meal' Louverture 'had a scrap of cheese, cut very carefully from the centre of the piece that was offered to him'.[22] Dessalines, the hero of Crête-à-Pierrot, highly disappointed by this turn of events, followed Christophe and submitted to Leclerc as well. Feeling betrayed by both Louverture and Christophe, he feigned devotion to Leclerc whilst demonstrating a much more real antipathy towards Louverture. He was already planning the push to expel the French and declare freedom for the colony. On 7 May, in one of several letters in which he exaggerated his success and downplayed his failure to deliver Bonaparte's plans, Leclerc nevertheless wrote: 'my present position is beautiful and brilliant . . . all the rebel chiefs have submitted.'[23]

The self-delusion implicit here is reflected in Leclerc's treatment of Louverture himself, who withdrew to his estate at Ennery but refused to assist Leclerc in his wider plans to return *cultivateurs* to work on the plantations. There is no evidence that he continued to plot in any way, but Leclerc – already frustrated at the compromises he had been forced to make regarding Bonaparte's orders – remained highly suspicious of his every move. Aware of Louverture's tactical brilliance, it is likely Leclerc thought his opponent was lying low, waiting for a change in the weather and the associated onset of tropical diseases to relaunch his attacks against the French. Acting on Leclerc's orders, General Jean-Baptiste Brunet sent Louverture a letter on 7 June 1802, inviting him to meet at his headquarters to discuss troop movements. Louverture was warned by those close to him that he risked arrest, but he went all the same, accompanied only a small group of guards drawn from among his remaining men. Brunet and Louverture talked briefly, then the French officer withdrew, allowing a party of grenadiers to enter the building and, with minimal resistance, to arrest the Haitian leader. Louverture was restrained, his family and close staff were also arrested the following day, and his house was ransacked.

The motivations underpinning Louverture's submission to arrest have been the subject of considerable speculation. Pamphile de Lacroix considered that he was genuinely hoodwinked in a moment of gullibility – although, as Madison Smartt Bell adds, this explanation relies on evidence of 'vanity, and a susceptibility to flattery which nothing else in his whole career suggests'.[24] C.L.R. James saw in this episode evidence of the hubris that characterised Louverture's final years, and of the sense of infallibility with which this is associated. Aimé Césaire follows the logic of this analysis a certain distance, but then claims that Louverture, at last aware of the flaws in his conduct, committed an intentionally self-sacrificial act in order to clear the way for the final stage of the War of Independence. Louverture was rushed to Cap Français and forced to embark on the frigate *La Créole*, then transferred to *Le Héros*, the vessel that would take him to France. As he climbed on board, he spoke to the ship's captain Savary, making what has subsequently become one of his most famous statements: 'In overthrowing me, you have cut down in San Domingo only the trunk of the tree of liberty. It will spring up again by the roots for they are numerous and deep.'[25]

Crossing the Atlantic in Reverse

In *Monsieur Toussaint*, his dramatic reflection on Louverture's imprisonment in the mountains of the Jura in eastern France, the Martinican author Édouard Glissant describes his protagonist crossing the Atlantic in reverse, seemingly overturning the traditional vector of the Middle Passage.[26] The journey to France was, however, far from being a triumphant one, not least because the Haitian revolutionary leader was now the prisoner of Bonaparte. It seemed that his achievements had been entirely undermined by Leclerc's expedition, the aim of which was now clear: to restore slavery and bring Saint-Domingue back under colonial rule. Philippe Girard describes how Louverture, undoubtedly influenced by his father's own accounts of the Middle Passage, greatly feared sea travel, and we can only imagine the impact that incarceration and the Atlantic crossing had on the man who until recently had served as Governor-General of Saint-Domingue.[27] On 12 July 1802, after a 26-day journey, the *Héros* entered the port of Brest on the western tip of Brittany. On board, still in the clothing he had been wearing when he was arrested, was Toussaint Louverture, accompanied by his wife, sons, several other family members, and his servant Mars Plaisir. His sons Isaac and Placide, whose education in France had been disrupted by their return to Haiti with Leclerc's troops the previous year, now found themselves in radically different circumstances. After a month in the port, during which the vessel cleared quarantine, the family was split up, with Placide sent to Belle-Île, Louverture's wife, sons Isaac and Saint-Jean, and nieces to Bayonne. In the letters he wrote during his incarceration, it is the fate of his family, about whom he received no news, that often preoccupied Louverture, especially that of Placide who had fought alongside him against Leclerc and whose punishment he feared as a result.

Imprisonment in the Château de Joux

Louverture himself was held briefly in Brest, but Bonaparte, having considered but quickly rejected the idea of a court-martial, decided to imprison him without trial, along with Mars Plaisir, as far away as possible from the coast – and by extension as far as possible from Saint-Domingue itself. Leclerc had recommended such a course of action, anxious about the continued influence of Louverture over the course of events in Haiti: 'You cannot possibly keep Toussaint at too great a distance from the sea, nor put him in a prison too sure; that man has fanaticized his country to such a point that his presence here would set it on fire all over again.'[28] It was decided that he would be held in the relatively inaccessible Château de Joux, in the glacial mountains of the Jura, but this meant a hazardous journey across France, in part through areas where the authorities still feared the potential threat of the counter-revolutionary *chouans*. Louverture was transported, therefore, in a closed carriage, accompanied by an armed guard. The Haitian general and diplomat Auguste Nemours, whom C.L.R. James consulted when he was writing *The Black Jacobins*, describes in detail the journey across France: there were several false alarms along the way, with those guarding Louverture clearly paranoid that attempts would be made to liberate their prisoner.[29]

Avoiding Paris and stopping only briefly in the cities along the way, the cortege arrived at Besançon on 22 August 1802, and after a brief stay in the nearby town of Pontarlier, Louverture was transferred to Joux the following day. He had reached the final earthly stage of his revolutionary life: the man famed for moving unimpeded around Haiti, appearing and disappearing unexpectedly, was now held in a confined space where, within months, he would die alone.

Louverture describes, in his memoir written at Joux, the helplessness of his situation: 'They have sent me to France naked as a worm; they have seized my property and my papers; they have spread the most atrocious calumnies on my account. Is this not to cut off someone's legs and order him to walk? Is it not to cut out his tongue and tell him to talk? Is it not to bury a man alive?'[30] In seeking to erase Louverture from public memory, both in the Caribbean and in France, Bonaparte achieved, however, the opposite result; mistreatment and neglect of his prisoner would, in time, only add to Louverture's renown as the Haitian revolutionary resisted his captor's tyranny to the end and defended his achievements during the revolutionary period.

The prison to which Louverture was sent had been constructed in a highly strategic location back in the eleventh century, and progressively extended over a period of centuries, including a major remodelling by Vauban. A final building project by Joseph Joffre in the 1870s, integrating the château into the defences of the Maginot line, created the site that can still be visited today. By the time Louverture was imprisoned there, the core of the fortress was already surrounded by five walls and three moats. A border fort halfway between Besançon and Lausanne, the site overlooks the mountain pass known as the Cluse de Pontarlier, part of what was once the contested borderland between France and Switzerland. Successive French governments used Joux as a prison between the seventeenth and nineteenth centuries, but it was Bonaparte who, under the Empire, used it most extensively to incarcerate those hostile to his regime. The prison, declared a national monument in 1949, is now a major tourist site, drawing visitors to its striking location, architectural eclecticism and anecdotes relating to its roster of celebrity prisoners. Guides now regale tourists with the story of Berthe de Joux, discovered *in flagrante* by her husband as he returned from the Crusades, and condemned to captivity in a cell whose only view was onto her lover's decomposing remains. Long before he became an early leader of the French Revolution, the Count of Mirabeau was imprisoned here too, held under a *lettre de cachet* supposedly arranged by his father to protect him from his debtors; Heinrich von Kleist, captured on suspicion of being a German spy, was held at Joux in 1807; but the most prominent inmate remains Louverture himself, whose cell has become a focus of pilgrimage for Haitian visitors and others from across the African diaspora.[31]

Although the Château de Joux was renowned as a secure location, at the time of Louverture's arrival it had recently been used to hold counter-revolutionary leaders from the uprising in the Vendée, whose escape had plunged the prison authorities into chaos. Security had been further tightened as a result, and the conditions faced by the Haitian revolutionary leader were devastatingly harsh ones. At an altitude of over 1,000 metres, high in the Jura mountains, Joux was cold and dark, providing a deliberately alienating contrast to the environment to which Louverture was accustomed in the Caribbean. The château – and more particularly the cell in which Louverture was held – has now become a prominent *lieu de mémoire*, repeatedly represented in Haitian literature (in the work of prominent authors such as Oswald Durand and Vendenasse Ducasse), but it also serves as a symbolic site of Caribbean memory more widely. The cell also features more generally in the literature relating to Louverture: in his 1802 sonnet, Wordsworth imagines his subject alone in 'some deep dungeon's earless den', and it is this isolation that Édouard Glissant would describe 150 years later in his play *Monsieur Toussaint*, a dramatisation of Louverture's final days in which the cell is populated by spectral figures from his past, holding the prisoner to account, questioning his motives, but ultimately celebrating the vision for the liberation of the Americas that underpinned his revolutionary struggle. Glissant writes: 'There is no fixed frontier between the universe of the prison and the lands of the Caribbean island', and his erasure of spatial distances underlines the symbolic value that Joux has acquired: a monument to the victims of Napoleonic brutality and the unflinching harshness of slavery, it is also – as its inclusion in Aimé Césaire's *Notebook of a Return to my Native Land* makes clear, celebrating the place where 'Negritude stood up for the first time' – a site of anti-colonial opposition and of the persistent resistance of the enslaved to their ongoing incarceration, whatever form that might take. In his essay collection *What the Twilight Says*, Derek Walcott describes the lack of monuments in the Caribbean, and dwells on the problematic nature of Henri Christophe's citadel: 'a monument to egomania, more than a strategic castle; an effort to reach God's height.'[32] Joux serves in many ways as its antithesis, the place in which a revolutionary hero was humiliated and left to die. It is a foundational site not just for Haitian national identity, but also for Caribbean identity more generally.

Louverture was incarcerated in a damp cell partly submerged in the rock, the window of which was almost entirely bricked up, meaning that he was deprived of light. His initial jailer was Baille, who reported regularly to the local prefect, who in turn communicated directly with the minister of police in Paris. In an act of humiliation, the prisoner was stripped of his military uniform and forced to wear civilian clothes. Subject to regular searches, he was deprived of his watch and money, so he would not be able to bribe his guards, and also saw any writing materials withdrawn in an attempt to prevent his efforts to communicate with government officials. When Baille was replaced by a more officious governor Amiot at the beginning of 1803, this surveillance increased, and was also extended to nocturnal searches aimed at increasing Louverture's discomfort. The damp and cold exacerbated his rheumatism, and he suffered from fever and headaches throughout his incarceration. Amiot in addition imposed a strict regime of solitude and silence, possible after Louverture's servant Mars Plaisir had been transferred to another prison. The prisoner's health was rapidly in decline, in part as a result of the deprivation of sufficiently warm clothing, food and firewood that the new jailer also imposed. In C.L.R. James's terms: 'Bonaparte decided to kill him by ill-treatment, cold and starvation',[33] and as Louverture's time in prison was prolonged, so his conditions deteriorated further. Finally, medical attention was withdrawn, and it became increasingly apparent that he would not be able to resist these circumstances for much longer. Given the prisoner's growing fragility, it became increasingly apparent this harsh regime was imposed not on the grounds of security, but to maximise Louverture's suffering. Philippe Girard comments incisively on the slippage between the official record and more personal narrative of the revolutionary's decline: 'Louverture's captivity,' he writes, 'is well documented in the official French records archived in Besançon and Vincennes, but most of these sources merely record petty fights over receipts. There is no way to reconstruct Louverture's last inner battles.'[34] This is true across his final months, for the understanding of which we have no trace of the prisoner's own voice and need to resort to the accounts of others. We do still have, however, access to a remarkable document produced by Louverture in the early months of his captivity, a memoir drafted as an act of self-justification, as a defence of his legacy, and as a petitioning of Bonaparte from whom the Haitian revolutionary requested a public trial at which he could attempt to clear his name.

In response to Louverture's petitioning of Napoleon, the First Consul had sent his general Caffarelli to interrogate the prisoner shortly after his transfer to Joux. During a six-day stay at the château, Caffarelli sought information on the revolutionary leader's conduct during Leclerc's campaign, and also questioned him on his earlier dealing with the British and in particular with Maitland (now promoted to the rank of General). Despite the inevitable distortions they contain, Caffarelli's notes on their discussions reveal that, despite his physical fragility, Louverture maintained a consistent account of his actions during the Revolution and – far from seeking forgiveness – defended his record for restoring prosperity to Saint-Domingue. His priority was to defend himself against Leclerc, providing what he calls in his opening sentence of his memoir 'an exact account of my conduct'.[35] He seems to contrast his loyalty and professionalism with what he saw as the French general's deeply underhand behaviour. Caffarelli left without any of the information he had hoped to obtain, in particular relating to Louverture's alleged treasure, but was given to pass on to Bonaparte a copy of Louverture's memoir, a document of around 16,000 words produced with the support of the governor Baille, whose (relatively) more benevolent regime the prisoner had enjoyed in the first months of his incarceration.

Four manuscript versions of the memoir have survived, three written by a secretary, but one – correcting factual errors in the other copies – in Louverture's own hand.[36] The prisoner was writing in harsh conditions and in a language that was almost certainly, after Fon and Haitian Kreyòl, his third. The handwriting is hard to decipher and the grammar lacking in accuracy, but the document remains an invaluable one: a first-person, eyewitness account of the final years of the Haitian Revolution produced by one of its key protagonists. It is also a very rare example in French-language literature of a slave narrative. In the memoir, Louverture deliberately skates over his early life and indeed says little directly about the first decade of the revolution. His principal focus is on February 1802, the arrival of Leclerc's expedition, and the events that followed this. He seeks above all to denounce the conduct of Leclerc, and defend his own actions, including the drafting of the 1801 constitution, presented as an act not of hostility but of loyalty towards France. A brief section follows, outlining his campaign against the British, again seeking to stress his commitment to France, and the text ends with a petition for Bonaparte's mercy.

The memoir is as much a literary as a political document, and the contemporary reader has to negotiate the balance between historical narrative and heartfelt attempts at self-justification. The narrative voice of the text vacillates between, on the one hand, that of a senior army officer and politician indignant at what he sees as an unjust fall from grace, and on the other, of a family man devastated to have been separated from his loved ones, about whose fate he had no information. The document had no tangible impact, not least because Bonaparte had already decided to remain wholly inflexible towards the Haitian revolutionary as part of his commitment to reversing the effects of the events of the previous decade in Saint-Domingue.

Receiving no response to his memoir, Louverture wrote two further letters to Bonaparte in October 1802, requesting clemency for himself and his family, but from the start of 1803, Amiot's harsh treatment of his prisoner accelerated the revolutionary leader's decline. The governor refused to request medical assistance without explicit authorisation from his superiors, even though Louverture had developed a serious cough and also suffered from crippling stomach pains. On 8 April 1803, the governor reported that, at half past eleven that morning, while bringing him his daily ration of food, he had discovered Louverture dead, 'sitting in his chair by the fire'. There have been suggestions that Louverture was poisoned or that Amiot deliberately starved him to death, but as Philippe Girard explains succinctly: 'Louverture died because his body was old and cold. He also died because his heart was broken.'[37] An autopsy was carried out, with the cause of death recorded as apoplexy and pneumonia. Louverture's body was buried in the crypt beneath the former chapel, where soldiers in the fort were also buried, but the building was demolished when the site was expanded in the late 1870s, and the revolutionary's remains are now mixed in with the foundations of extended walls. Joux has acquired the status of a sacred site for Haitian visitors, reflected in Auguste Nemours's dramatic claim that the cell in the château can be equated with Christ's cross and Prometheus's rock as global sites of suffering and sacrifice.[38] The lack of a marked grave has created difficulties, not least when proposals have been made on several occasions for the transfer of Louverture's remains to the French Panthéon. A symbolic crate of soil, taken from the area of the Château de Joux where the revolutionary was believed to have been buried, was given to Haiti on the 180th anniversary of the revolutionary's death in 1983, but the contrast with Bonaparte's tomb in les Invalides is a striking one. Incarceration at Joux had been an attempt to strip Louverture of any revolutionary power and influence, and to erase him from popular memory. This suppression failed, both in the short term as the processes begun by Louverture in Haiti continued to run their course, and in the longer term, as the revolutionary's afterlives reveal his irrepressible potential to inspire future generations in their own revolutionary struggles.

The Rendezvous of Victory

'There is no drama,' writes C.L.R. James, 'like the drama of history. Toussaint died on April 7th, 1803 and Bonaparte must have thought that half the battle against San Domingo was now won. But in Toussaint's last hours his comrades in arms, ignorant of his fate, were drafting the declaration of independence.'[39] By the time Louverture was facing his lonely death at Joux in Spring 1803, the struggle for emancipation he had initiated had over the previous six months erupted in earnest once more. James explains the reasons for this reignition of resistance: 'The news of Toussaint's arrest came like a cold shock to the whole population. Whatever Toussaint had done, he stood for liberty.'[40] As they understood the extent of Leclerc's plans to re-impose slavery, the generals who had recently surrendered to the leader of Bonaparte's expeditionary force regrouped, and their resistance to the French was reignited. News of Bonaparte's decision to maintain slavery in Martinique had initially reached Saint-Domingue in August 1802, and this was supplemented by an indication the next month that there were similar intentions in Guadeloupe, following the crushing of the revolt there, led by Louis Delgrès in May of the same year. Key members of Leclerc's forces – such as Alexandre Pétion – began to turn against him, and any power he had to challenge these rebels was further diminished when two of the most senior generals in Louverture's army, Dessalines and Christophe, also changed sides and resolved again to resist the French. Pressure from the rebel forces was complemented by devastation caused by yellow fever, which killed many French troops and also caused Leclerc's own death in November 1802. His successor General Rochambeau unleashed a brutal riposte, slaughtering members of the free coloured population, drowning his prisoners (including Louverture's godfather Pierre Baptiste), importing dogs to hunt down rebel troops, and seeking to suppress any opposition to his attempts to re-impose slavery. The result was, not surprisingly, a galvanisation of resistance, meaning that a common front was forged between the black and mixed-race populations in Saint-Domingue. In this context, Dessalines emerged as the natural leader of the campaign to expel the French from the colony once and for all. As C.L.R. James notes:

> Dessalines was a one-sided genius, but he was the man for this crisis, not Toussaint. He gave blow for blow. When Rochambeau put to death 500 at Le Cap and buried them in a large hole dug while they waited for execution, Dessalines raised gibbets of branches and hanged 500 for Rochambeau and the whites of Le Cap to see.[41]

Louverture had maintained a hope, subsequently dashed, that Saint-Domingue would be able to exist with relative autonomy as part of some sort of French Commonwealth; he had, as a result, believed in the possibility of co-operation among the ethnic groups present in the colony. Dessalines entertained no such illusions, and was committed not only to the defeat of the French, but also to avoiding the reestablishment of slavery, to the eradication if necessary of any white presence in the country. Whereas Louverture had been the diplomatic and tactical precursor to Haitian emancipation, Dessalines would prove himself to be the country's liberator. Burying his differences with the coloured generals, to whom he had recently been opposed in the so-called 'War of the Knives', he sought – not always successfully – to forge a common front against the French. This is symbolised in his dramatic tearing of the white strip from the tricolour, creating a flag with just two stripes, red and blue, reflecting the alliance of the black and coloured populations. As war between France and Britain broke out again in Spring 1803, no further French troops could be sent to the Caribbean, and the British began to support Dessalines's forces, not least by blockading Haiti's ports. Rochambeau lashed out, terrorising the coloured population in particular, but the days of French Saint-Domingue were numbered. In April 1803, as Louverture died at Joux, Bonaparte ceded Louisiana to the United States, effectively abandoning his ambitions for an empire in the Americas. The French withdrew from Port-au-Prince in October 1803, and left the colony after their defeat by Dessalines at Vertières the following month. Fifty thousand French troops had been killed in this ill-fated attempt to overturn the revolutionary process and re-impose slavery on Saint-Domingue.[42] Over a decade later, in exile on St Helena, Bonaparte would admit that this campaign had been one of his greatest errors.

A preliminary proclamation of independence, still using the colonial name Saint-Domingue, was published on 29 November 1803, signed by Dessalines, Christophe and Clerveaux. A more radical version, signed by Dessalines alone, appeared on 1 January 1804. Adopting the former Taino name for Hispaniola, Haiti, the new constitution signalled nonetheless a rupture and new departure: 'Peace to our neighbours. But anathema to the French name. Hatred eternal to France. This is our cry.'[43] Girard suggests that 'under Dessalines's definition of citizenship, put forth in Article 14 of his 1805 constitution, to be Haitian was to be black . . . his extreme racial agenda betrayed, in the eyes of many, the egalitarian ideals of the Haitian Revolution'.[44] In fact, as Robin Blackburn notes:

Colour distinctions, especially between black and mulatto, continued to be important but had no legal force, and citizenship extended to all, including Poles and Germans who had defected from the French army. The term *blanc* (white), as employed in Haiti, does not describe a person by reference to the colour of their skin. Instead it became – as it remains to this day – the vernacular term for any foreigner, even if they are Jamaicans or Brazilians of dark complexion.[45]

Such a radical understanding of race and citizenship perhaps stands testament to how, as Blackburn notes, 'the racialized structure of exploitation fostered a countervailing solidarity, since only those of African descent were enslaved'. The popular Kreyòl saying *tou moun se moun* (everyone is a person) – a manifestly humanist position – perhaps echoed African notions of *Ubuntu*, signifying that a person is a person through other people.[46] Historians have often sought to contrast Louverture and Dessalines, but when the latter promulgated his 1805 constitution, traces of the Precursor were readily apparent: a commitment to the abolition of slavery in perpetuity was combined with authoritarian aspects of the 'Louverturian' state, such as the continuation of forced labour as a means of ensuring independence. Both in Haiti as well as in a more global frame, the afterlives of the revolutionary were becoming increasingly apparent.

6

. . . One and All: 1804–

The Impact of the Haitian Revolution

Before discussing, in conclusion, the ongoing evolution of the afterlives of Louverture himself, it is worth briefly reflecting on the place of the Haitian Revolution within wider contemporary discussions about slavery and abolition. David Geggus, who has done more than any other contemporary historian to advance scholarly understanding of the complexities and intricacies of the Haitian Revolution, notes that it 'freed about half a million people in 1793, and perhaps another 110,000 the following year, when the French Republic (temporarily) extended emancipation to Guadeloupe and Guyane', so liberating about one-third to 40 per cent of the Caribbean slave population from bondage. Geggus then counterposes the Haitian Revolution to 'the British emancipation act of 1833', which 'freed fully half of the remaining population, some 665,000 slaves', drawing the conclusion that 'metropolitan abolitionism contributed at least as much as Caribbean revolution during this period to freeing slaves and to shrinking the regional slave population'.[1] However, such an argument implicitly downplays the impact that the Haitian Revolution – or the threat or fear of it engulfing the wider Caribbean region – made on 'metropolitan abolitionism', including in the British context in the aftermath of Haiti's declaration of independence. Geggus accepts that the Haitian Revolution 'perhaps' could be seen to have influenced the Jacobin decision to end slavery throughout the French Empire in 1794, but seems reluctant to concede, even 'perhaps', that the decision of the British to abandon their highly profitable slave trade in 1807, only three years after Haiti's declaration of independence in 1804, was due to the 'threat of a good example' that Haiti now posed across the Caribbean. Challenging the likes of Geggus, scholars like Robin Blackburn and Gelian Matthews have pointed to how the British state's decision to abolish colonial slavery throughout the British Empire in 1833 was shaped by slave revolts in the British Caribbean in the aftermath of Haiti in Barbados (1816), Demerara (1823) and most critically in Jamaica (1831–32).[2]

Indeed, what is undeniable is the inspiration the Haitian Revolution represented for those seeking emancipation from slavery in other slave societies across the Americas and especially in the Caribbean region, a minority of whom led their own uprisings to try and spread the revolution accordingly. In the British Caribbean, for example, during 1791–92, hundreds of enslaved people in Jamaica were involved in unrest, while hundreds more took part in the 'Second Maroon War' from 1795–96. In 1795, there were also revolts in Dominica and Dutch Demerara, 'the Second Carib War' erupted in St Vincent, while the Fédon rebellion in Grenada from 1795–96 was followed in 1796–97 by the 'Brigands' War', involving thousands of enslaved people on St Lucia. In 1801, hundreds of enslaved people in Tobago were involved in a Christmas plot.[3] After the Haitian Revolution had won victory in 1804, the following year in Trinidad, enslaved Africans planned their own revolt, again around Christmas time, in the French-owned plantations near the capital of Port of Spain. They organised themselves into bands and met in a ceremony at night which had clear echoes of Bois Caïman:

> Pan nous ka mange
> C'est viande beké;
> Di vin nous ka boué
> C'est sang beké.
> He! St. Domingo, songé St. Domingo!

> (The bread you are eating is the white man's flesh, the wine you are drinking is the white man's blood. Hey, Saint-Domingue, remember Saint-Domingue!)[4]

In Cuba, in 1812, Ada Ferrer notes that the leader of the Aponte rebellion, 'the most widespread and ambitious conspiracy in Cuba in this period . . . was a free black carpenter who recruited slaves and free people, showing them pictures in a book that he had made, which included images of scenes and people from Saint-Domingue'. The book included images of Louverture and Christophe.[5] Further testament to the inspiration of the Haitian Revolution for a subsequent slave revolt came with the 'Bussa rebellion' in the British colony of Barbados in 1816. Here one rebel, James Bowland, had talked of a place where the enslaved had fought and won freedom that he called 'Mingo', while one literate enslaved woman who worked as a domestic in the big house on the Simmons estate, Nanny Grigg, had been spreading the rumour throughout 1815 that all were to be free on New Year's Day 1816. When that day came and went without emancipation, Grigg became more militant, and as one other rebel later confessed, 'About a fortnight after New-year's day, she said the Negroes were to be freed on Easter-Monday, and the only way to get it was to fight for it, otherwise they would not get it; and the way they were to do, was to set fire, as that was the way they did in Saint Domingo'.[6]

Geggus has suggested that 'one might also further argue that the final success of British antislavery was the more significant development in that, as precedent and example, it was more relevant to the future demise of American slavery than was the Haitian Revolution'.[7] Again, such an argument implicitly downplays the inspiration the Haitian Revolution provided for those at the very forefront of fighting American slavery – the enslaved of America itself. Gabriel Prosser, a literate enslaved blacksmith born around 1776, was inspired by the Haitian Revolution when he planned a slave revolt in Richmond, Virginia in 1800, for which he was executed together with twenty-four of his followers when the plans were unfortunately leaked in advance. In 1822, Denmark Vesey, who was born into slavery around 1767 in St Thomas (a Danish Caribbean colony, hence his name), and had experienced slavery in colonial Saint-Domingue himself during 1781 for a period, planned to organise an insurrection in Charleston, South Carolina. Vesey had, for obvious reasons, been inspired by the Haitian Revolution while it was taking place, and even though he obtained his own liberty in Charleston in 1800 by winning the local lottery, he avidly studied its history as a guide to action in preparation.

Nat Turner, who led the single most consequential slave uprising in the history of the United States, in Virginia in 1831, was also inspired by the Haitian Revolution. One contemporary account noted Turner visited and associated with blacks on plantations in the lead-up to the rebellion, and 'represented to them the happy effects which had attended the united efforts of their brethren in St. Domingo, and elsewhere, and encouraged them with the assurance that a similar effort on their part, could not fail to produce a similar effect, and not only restore them to liberty but would produce them wealth and ease!'[8] As for the demise of American slavery, the abolitionist John Brown also studied the Haitian Revolution carefully before waging his own slave war, while the historian Matthew Clavin has tracked the inspiration of Haiti for those blacks fighting in the American Civil War, noting for example that the company nickname of the Fifty-Fourth Massachusetts Regiment, one of the first official units of African-Americans, about a quarter of whom had been formerly enslaved, was the 'Toussaint Guards'.[9]

Finally, the inspiration the Haitian Revolution provided for other anti-colonial and national liberation struggles needs to be registered briefly, for after all, as *The Times* had already noted on 1 January 1802, '[a] Black State in the Western Archipelago is utterly incompatible with the system of all European colonisation'.[10] As James noted in *The Black Jacobins*, the Haitian Revolution 'brought into the world more than the abolition of slavery'.

> When Latin Americans saw that small and insignificant Haiti could win and keep independence they began to think that they ought to be able to do the same. [In 1816] Pétion, the ruler of Haiti, nursed back to health the sick and defeated [Simon] Bolívar, gave him money, arms and a printing press to help in the campaign which ended in the freedom of the Five States.[11]

In Ireland, there was an identification among many with the cause of enslaved black people. The black abolitionist Olaudah Equiano had made an impact when he toured in 1790, and the 1798 rebellion led by the United Irishmen, though brutally crushed, was itself one of the great Atlantic Revolutions of the period. As Kevin

Whelan notes, 'many exiled United Irishmen had joined maroon communities in Jamaica in 1799', as after 'they were "incautiously drafted into the regiments"', they 'promptly fled to the mountains to fight with maroons and French against the British'.[12] Peter Linebaugh and Marcus Rediker record the outcome: 'after the rebellion of 1798, the slaughter was vast: thirty thousand, far in excess of the number dead in Robespierre's Terror'. They cite a description of a letter from Jamaica in 1799, which was sent to Castlereagh, then Chief Secretary of Ireland,

A vast number of United Irishmen, transported from this kingdom, have been landed there, and incautiously drafted into the regiments on that service. As soon as they got arms into their hands, they deserted, and fled into the mountains, where they have been joined by large bodies of natives and such of the French as were in the island. There have already been some engagements between this party and the King's troops; several have been killed and wounded on both sides.[13]

As Kevin Whelan notes, there is clear evidence that many United Irishmen were inspired by the Haitian Revolution, and Louverture's leadership in particular:

The veteran United Irishman James Napper Tandy, although based in France, disapproved of the ruthless French suppression of the Toussaint insurrection: 'We are all of the same family, black and white, the work of the same creator.' Toussaint's struggle engaged the attention of the Irish 'rhyming weaver and United Irishman, James Orr (1770–1816) of Ballycarry, County Antrim', whose anti-slavery poems included 'Toussaint's Farewell to St Domingo' (1805), 'The Dying African' (1806) and 'The Persecuted Negro' (1809). Another United Irishman, John Swiney, named one of his sons Toussaint in 1808.[14]

The Afterlives of Louverture

Even during his lifetime, Louverture himself had been subject to extensive processes of representation, ranging from hagiography to demonisation. In Britain, for example, David Geggus notes that 'the *Annual Register* for 1802 described him as the major public figure of the year, and a great man', but also that William Cobbett – remembered today as a voice of radicalism, but in this period at least also 'a staunch supporter of slavery and the slave trade, and virulently racist' – hoped the French would hang 'the silly, wavering, cowardly Toussaint'.[15] Contemporary biographers tended to denigrate his character, a tendency most clear in Dubroca's 1802 account of his life, but these negative accounts are counterbalanced by the positive eyewitness narratives of writers such as Marcus Rainsford, cited already above, who met Louverture while in Saint-Domingue in 1799 and provides a deeply human portrait of him. Even a detractor such as the Haitian historian Beaubrun Ardouin saw the manner of Louverture's death as instrumental in the creation of his posthumous reputation:

Toussaint Louverture not only had been struck by the hand of man, he had been struck especially by that divine Providence whose sacred laws he had so ignored. [. . .] [Providence] desired that [Toussaint] expiate in a dungeon all his wrongs, all the crimes he had committed while all-powerful, in order to present us an example to his contemporaries, to posterity . . . [16]

The active instrumentalisation of the Haitian revolutionary began soon after his death, particularly in the context of the abolition of slavery as this played itself out across a range of national contexts. Louverture provided abolitionists with a striking model of the potential of the enslaved to manage themselves after emancipation. Often preferred to his contemporaries Christophe and Dessalines, he offered an apparent illustration of education, religious faith and moderation. This was a reading reflected in the tendency to disassociate Louverture from the violence of the early stages of the Haitian Revolution and the final stages of the War of Independence. Such a representation stresses unquestioningly the case he sought to make in his own memoir of his consistent loyalty to France, twisted on occasion to indicate dependency on the coloniser as well as a commitment to a gradualist approach to freedom. In such a context, Louverture's lack of contact with the formerly enslaved masses, presented by C.L.R. James as his tragic flaw, was seen as a virtue, with the revolutionary aspects of his actions accordingly minimised and his character conscripted to the more conservative strands of abolitionist thought.

The British abolitionist James Stephen wrote a life of Louverture in 1802, and used this to contrast a positive view of his subject against a negative portrait of Bonaparte, in an attempt to rally the support of his country for the Haitian revolutionaries against the French. When he rewrote the volume in 1814, it was dedicated to Alexander I of Russia, and Stephen attempted to produce a flattering portrait of Louverture with whom, seeking to win over Russian support at the Congress of Vienna, he hoped the Czar would identify:

> That illustrious African well deserved the exalted names of Christian, Patriot and Hero. He was a devout worshipper of his God, and a successful defender of his invaded country. He was the victorious enemy, at once, and the contrast of Napoleon Buonaparte, whose arms he repelled, and whose pride he humbled, not more by the strength of his military genius, than by the moral influence of his amiable and virtuous character.[17]

The 'moral influence of his amiable and virtuous character' was also a theme in the Victorian radical-leaning George Dibdin Pitt's blackface minstrel play staged in London in 1846, *Toussaint L'Ouverture, or The Black Spartacus*. Though only Act I survived, it has been described by Hazel Waters as 'an uneasy mix of comedy and melodrama' that depicted Louverture's main concern as 'saving his owner's family from the black revolution'.[18] The theme of Louverture's 'virtuous character' also shaped the Reverend John R. Beard's *Life of Toussaint L'Ouverture: The Negro Patriot of Hayti*, published in 1853 on the fiftieth anniversary of Louverture's death, an important and valuable work which nonetheless, C.L.R. James noted, made Louverture 'out to be an admirable example of a Protestant clergyman turned revolutionary'.[19]

In France, where the second abolition of slavery occurred in 1848, the role of Louverture in abolitionist debate was more ambiguous, not least because of the French reluctance to recognise Haitian independence until the country accepted to pay a huge debt in exchange in 1825. The Romantic poet and dramatist Lamartine nevertheless devoted a relatively melodramatic play to Louverture, performed with popular success on the Parisian stage in the aftermath of abolition in 1848, and the abolitionist Victor Schoelcher later devoted a biography to Louverture, one of the first to draw extensively on contemporary archival sources and offer a more nuanced portrait of his subject, explaining negative aspects of his character with reference to enslavement in his early years, and seeing apparent disloyalty to France in the drafting of his 1801 constitution as evidence of a commitment to defending the prosperity of the colony and the gains of emancipation against the French.

In the United States, although W.E.B. Du Bois could rightly note that 'the role which the great Negro Toussaint, called L'Ouverture, played in the history of the United States has seldom been fully appreciated',[20] Louverture was nonetheless prominent in the writings of leading abolitionists during the nineteenth century, as one of what Matthew Clavin has called those 'resonant, polarizing, and ultimately subversive symbols' relating to the Haitian Revolution,[21] seen as both source of inspiration for African-American identity and a warning to those who would delay the ongoing processes of emancipation promised by the end of the Civil War. The Haitian Revolution became a staple of speeches by the likes of Wendell Phillips, whose eulogy to Louverture delivered in Boston in 1861 became particularly famous:

You may think me a fanatic tonight, for you read history, not with your eyes, but with your prejudices. But fifty years hence, when Truth gets a hearing, the Muse of History will put Phocion for the Greek, and Brutus for the Roman, Hampden for England, Fayette for France, choose Washington as the bright, consummate flower of our earlier civilization, and John Brown the ripe fruit of our noonday, then dipping her pen in the sunlight, will write in the clear blue, above them all, the name of the soldier, the statesman, the martyr, TOUSSAINT L'OUVERTURE.[22]

Through astounding rhetoric, Phillips tended to stress the exceptionalism of Louverture as well as his statesmanlike qualities, deploying his example for reformist rather than revolution-ary purposes. Louverture often served as an inspiration for more moderate African-American intellectuals and activists seeking inspi-rational figures for their assertion of black dignity and potential for self-government, such as the Reverend James Theodore Holly, who in 1857 declared the Haitian Revolution 'one of the noblest, grandest, and most justifiable outbursts against tyrannical oppression that is recorded on the pages of the world history'.[23] The formerly enslaved author and abolitionist William Wells Brown focused on the history of Haiti throughout his writings and drew inspiration from the figure of Louverture whom he contrasted favourably with statesmen in his own country: 'Toussaint liberated his countrymen; Washington enslaved a portion of his. When impartial history shall do justice to the St. Domingo revolution, the name of Toussaint L'Ouverture will be placed high upon the roll of fame.'[24]

This tendency continued into the later nineteenth century, when Frederick Douglass, who as an abolitionist would popularise the militant slogan 'Who would be free, themselves must strike the blow' (derived from Lord Byron's *Childe Harold's Pilgrimage*, 1812), had spent time in Haiti as US minister resident and consul general. Douglass devoted significant texts to Louverture, most notably in the context of his role as commissioner of the Haitian pavilion at the Chicago World's Fair of 1893. Here, the Haitian revolutionary is cited as an example of persistent commitment to the ideal of emancipation in a context of seemingly overwhelming hostility:

To have any just conception or measurement of the intelligence, solidarity and manly courage of the people of Haiti when under the lead of Toussaint L'Ouverture, and the dauntless Dessalines, you must remember what the conditions were by which they were surrounded; that all the neighbouring islands were slaveholding, and that to no one of all these islands could she look for sympathy, support and co-operation. She trod the wine press alone. Her hand was against the Christian world, and the hand of the Christian world was against her. Hers was a forlorn hope, and she knew that she must do or die.[25]

In the wider Caribbean, Louverture was also remembered and honoured by radicals as a heroic figure, a phenomenon historian Matthew J. Smith has recently traced. As Smith notes, Joseph Robert Love, a Bahamian medical doctor who had spent several years living in Haiti before settling in Jamaica in the 1890s, became a powerful orator and unrelenting activist for black political rights, and would give lectures on Louverture in Jamaica as an example of what could be achieved by black West Indians.[26] The *Daily Gleaner*, in a review of Love's lectures, crystallised the point with a line from William Wordsworth: 'What one is why may not millions be?'[27] This theme was taken up by the Jamaican Pan-Africanist Marcus Garvey, who saw himself as standing in a pantheon of black heroes including Louverture. In 1929 in a speech to some 15,000 supporters in Kingston, Jamaica, Garvey discussed the Haitian Revolution:

There the abolitionists did not agitate or the white philanthropists did not contribute to the cause of emancipating the people of that country. But there to the honour of their country and our race a black man fought for the liberty of his people – Toussaint L'Ouverture – the greatest Negro to ever come out of the West; because he was successful in leading in Santo Domingo an army which beat the trained soldiers of France and the trained soldiers of England.[28]

By 1929, Garvey's own movement was coming under sustained pressure from not only the American government and other European colonial authorities, but also from a new generation of black radicals who were inspired by the Russian Revolution of 1917 and the hope it represented of a world without exploitation and oppression, and were gravitating towards organisations associated with the Communist International. The socialist tradition of internationalism might be dated from Gracchus Babeuf's support for the Jacobins' decision to abolish slavery across the French empire on 4 February 1794 (16 Pluviôse an II), which he hailed as 'this benevolent decree which has broken the odious chains of our brothers the blacks'.[29]

The wider working-class movement would from its beginnings also take a place at the forefront of the abolitionist movement, though this would inevitably be a more contradictory and complex affair. In Britain, for example, despite working-class support for figures like William Cobbett, the London Corresponding Society showed support for abolitionists like Equiano during the 1790s, and a mass meeting was organised by radicals in Sheffield in April 1794 which voted unanimously against the slave trade and for 'a total Emancipation of the Negro Slaves', for 'wishing to be rid of the weight of oppression under which *we* groan, we are induced to compassionate those who groan also'.[30] Black radical figures like Robert Wedderburn, William Davidson and William Cuffay played leading roles in the British working class movement in the early nineteenth century.[31] As well as welcoming Cuffay as one of its leaders, as early as the 1830s Richard Oastler declared the causes of anti-slavery and the Chartist movement were 'one and the same'.[32] Karl Marx himself, and organisations such as the International Working Men's Association, continued this internationalist tradition in their opposition to racism and slavery, Marx famously noting in *Capital* that 'Labour cannot emancipate itself in the white skin where in the black it is branded'.[33]

Writing in May 1929 in *The Communist*, the black West Indian radical Cyril Briggs, born in colonial Nevis and active in socialist politics in the United States in the early twentieth century, wrote a famous profile of 'Negro Revolutionary Hero – Toussaint L'Ouverture'. As Briggs wrote, after quoting Wendell Phillips's famous eulogy:

> Wendell Phillips appraised Toussaint L'Ouverture according to the standards of his class and day. Today . . . there are different standards and the great Negro revolutionary takes his place with the revolutionary heroes and martyrs of the world proletariat . . . To the black and white revolutionary workers belong the tradition of Toussaint L'Ouverture. We must see to it that his memory is not wrapped in spices in the vaults of the bourgeoisie but is kept green and fresh as a tradition of struggle and an inspiration for the present struggle against the master class.

From 1915, Haiti itself had been under US military occupation, and so Briggs fittingly concluded his article by calling 'For the full emancipation of the Negro masses of the U.S.! For the liberation of

Haiti from the heels of United States Marines!'[34] This was a theme echoed by other black Communists during this period, such as the black Trinidadian radical George Padmore, who edited the *Negro Worker* in which he declared 'Down with American Imperialism! . . . Long live the spirit of Toussaint Louverture! Long live the independence of the Haitian people!'[35] In the interwar period, not least in the context of the US occupation of Haiti, which lasted until 1934, Toussaint Louverture once again more generally achieved a high level of prominence on both sides of the Atlantic and beyond. A key intervention in this period was the work written by George Padmore's boyhood friend C.L.R. James, *The Black Jacobins* (1938), the first account of the Revolution in the light of Marxist historiography but also – as reference to the book throughout this volume has made clear – a major biography of Louverture himself. James's interest in the revolutionary leader had initially led to a play staged in London with Paul Robeson in the lead role in 1936, *Toussaint Louverture: The Story of the Only Successful Slave Revolt in History.* Both drama and history reveal the ways in which the Haitian struggle for independence served as an inspiration and warning for those engaged in a series of contemporary political movements, most notably protesting against fascist Italy's invasion of Ethiopia in 1935, and developing the Pan-African movement that would become a major force in the emergence of anti-colonialism.

The memory of Toussaint Louverture, who had defeated European armies through a ruthless guerrilla war waged from the mountains of Haiti, took on new resonance for Pan-Africanist activists in organisations like the London-based International African Friends of Ethiopia (IAFE) led – amidst Mussolini's looming invasion – by C.L.R. James himself and the Jamaican Pan-Africanist Amy Ashwood Garvey.[36] At a public meeting of the IAFE, on 28 July 1935, 'Wordsworth's sonnet to the black hero of Haiti' was read out, while James put it to the meeting that should the Ethiopians find themselves unable to get to grips with the Italian colonial troops in conventional combat, 'we look to them to destroy their country rather than hand it over to the invader. Let them burn down Addis Ababa, let them poison their wells and water holes, let them destroy every blade of vegetation. Let them die free rather than live enslaved'.[37]

The Black Jacobins was one of several accounts of Louverture published during the period, including Percy Waxman's *The Black Napoléon: The Story of Toussaint L'Ouverture* (1930), but what was distinctive in James's interpretation was the ways in which the life of Louverture and his fellow revolutionary leaders was seen to contain metaphorical dimensions that transcend their immediate circumstances of the late-eighteenth- and early-nineteenth-century Caribbean. James's study of the power struggles that characterised the Revolution can be read also in the context of the political evolution of the Soviet Union in the 1920s and 1930s. It is not surprising, therefore, that Louverture featured in the work of Russian writers of the period, most notably in *The Black Consul* by Anatolii Vinogradov, an account of the French and Haitian Revolutions that concludes with an overview of Louverture's contributions to them. In cinema also, Eisenstein developed, over a number of years, plans for what would have been the first biopic of the revolutionary leader, a role in which he hoped to cast Robeson himself, a project he was eventually forced to abandon when it became apparent that political support had been withdrawn.[38]

The presence of Robeson in both James's drama and Eisenstein's ultimately aborted film underlines the continued importance of Haiti, and of Louverture in particular, in contemporary discussions of African-American identity. The Haitian pavilion at the Chicago World's Fair in 1893, the commissioner of which had been Frederick Douglass, had served as a key site for black Americans seeking to demand dignity and equality in the face of continuing racial discrimination. One of the centre pieces of the pavilion had been a bust of Louverture, and in the context of the Harlem Renaissance, he became the focus of further artistic representations, most notably in Jacob Lawrence's 41-panel *Toussaint L'Ouverture* series (1937–38), a striking visual account of Haiti's struggle for independence. In discussing the genesis of his work, Lawrence described the way in which he had regularly heard Louverture evoked by street corner orators in Harlem, and there is a clear sense that the Haitian revolutionary had by this stage achieved iconic status – alongside figures such as Harriet Tubman – in an African-American political pantheon. Robeson himself would regular evoke the Haitian Revolution in his speeches, including once dubbing Ho Chi Minh 'the Toussaint of Vietnam', 'the modern day Toussaint Louverture leading his people to freedom'.[39]

Indeed, in the post-war period, the Haitian Revolution would again serve as a source of inspiration for the anti-colonial movements seeking to draw on an earlier model of revolutionary success. Although in evidence in a range of contexts, not least sub-Saharan African and Latin America, where Louverture inspired work by authors as diverse as Bernard Dadié and Pablo Neruda, the revolutionary had a specific impact in debates around decolonisation and its afterlives in the Caribbean. As we have seen already, Aimé Césaire devoted a key passage of his 1939 poem *Notebook of a Return to my Native Land* to Louverture, and he returned to the revolutionary leader in a more substantial historical account of Haiti's liberation published in 1960. By that stage, the poet-politician had grown increasingly disillusioned by the departmentalisation to which Martinique had been subject in 1946 and of which at the time he had been one of the principal advocates. Césaire identifies clear parallels between his own struggles for equality with France and those attempted by Louverture, and sees a historical precedent for the failure of departmentalisation in the betrayal of the Haitian's leaders own efforts – dashed by Bonaparte – to create a French commonwealth in which there would be parity between France and Haiti.

At the same time as Césaire published his history, his fellow Martinican Édouard Glissant, then active in the movement agitating for autonomy of the French Antilles and French Guiana, produced the first of several versions of his play (cited above) about Louverture's captivity and death at Joux. A sympathetic portrayal of Louverture the man, the drama uses the prisoner's cell to stage an account of Haitian history before and during the Revolution, underlining its protagonist's creoleness and suggesting his centrality to a new conception of Caribbean identity that would break dependency on the Western metropoles and forge new solidarities across the region.

It is striking that as Césaire and Glissant were engaging with the revolutionary legacies of Louverture in the departmentalised Francophone Caribbean, writers in the Anglophone islands were also forging new connections with Haitian history in the context of their own transition to independence. The Barbadian George Lamming devoted a section of his essay collection *The Pleasures of Exile* (1960) to Louverture, and it was Lamming who encouraged C.L.R. James, recently returned to London after a prolonged period of political organising in the USA, to revisit *The Black Jacobins* and prepare a new edition of the work. When this appeared in 1963, James was heavily disillusioned by the independence process he had witnessed in his native Trinidad, where he had become a vocal critic of the Prime Minister, his former friend and collaborator Eric Williams. At the same time, however, he drew significant political inspiration from the Cuban Revolution of 1959, and wrote a significant appendix to his history, entitled 'From Toussaint L'Ouverture to Fidel Castro', in which he described a history of revolutionary struggle in the Caribbean:

> Toussaint Louverture and Fidel Castro led a revolutionary people . . . whatever its ultimate fate, the Cuban revolution marks the ultimate stage of a Caribbean quest for national identity. In a scattered series of disparate islands, the process consists of a series of uncoordinated periods of drift, punctuated by spurts, leaps and catastrophes. But the inherent movement is clear and strong.[40]

James identifies both in Louverture – 'the first and greatest of West Indians' – and in his revolutionary struggle the development of this 'Caribbean quest for national identity', a process begun in the 1790s under his leadership and still resonating in the later twentieth century and beyond.

James's connection of Louverture with Castro – and for that matter Robeson's connection of Louverture with Ho Chi Minh – raises an important issue that has come increasingly to the fore in the postcolonial world. This is also an issue that remains with us in the twenty-first century, one that James himself identified in *The Black Jacobins* as that of 'the change from the old to the new despotism' under Louverture as he made the transition from a revolutionary fighter into the statesman-like figurehead presiding over an emerging new system of class rule.[41] As David Geggus has suggested with respect to the Haitian Revolution:

far from being driven by 'democratic ideals', the revolution that grew out of the slave uprising was authoritarian from beginning to end . . . it is perfectly clear that the succession of gifted ex-slaves who emerged from the 1791 uprising and later took Saint-Domingue to independence never displayed the slightest regard for democracy. The politics of Toussaint Louverture, Jean-Jacques Dessalines, and Henry Christophe were unapologetically dictatorial.[42]

Or as Girard suggests of Louverture, 'enlightened dictatorship was his model, not the Enlightenment'.[43] One is tempted to respond to Geggus and Girard here by quoting Engels, writing in defence of the Paris Commune of 1871, which was being charged with being 'authoritarian', as it did not put 'the abolition of authority' as its first order of the day:

Have these gentlemen ever seen a revolution? A revolution is certainly the most authoritarian thing there is; it is the act whereby one part of the population imposes its will upon the other part by means of rifles, bayonets and cannon – authoritarian means, if such there be at all; and if the victorious party does not want to have fought in vain, it must maintain this rule by means of the terror which its arms inspire in the reactionists. Would the Paris Commune have lasted a single day if it had not made use of this authority of the armed people against the bourgeois?[44]

In fact, in a sense, the Haitian Revolution was actually *profoundly democratic* in terms of its struggle for national self-determination in the fact of colonial domination.

Moreover, we contend that 'enlightened absolutism' would probably be a more accurate description of Louverture's rule. As James noted:

Personal industry, social morality, public education, religious toleration, free trade, civic pride, racial equality, this ex-slave strove according to his lights to lay their foundations in the new State. In all his proclamations, laws and decrees he insisted on moral principles, the necessity for work, respect for law and order, pride in San Domingo, veneration for France. He sought to lift the people to some understanding of the duties and responsibilities of freedom and citizenship. It was the propaganda of a dictatorship, but not for base personal ends . . . No doubt the poor sweated and were backward so that the new ruling class might thrive. But at least they too were better off than they had been.[45]

Most critically, Louverture himself had about at best one year without warfare to try to govern and build a society amidst the ashes and ruins of an eighteenth-century slave society largely destroyed by the revolutionary upheaval. To expect him or any other Haitian revolutionary leader even to try to construct any kind of democratic society *in this period* would be utterly ahistorical – not least since the only contemporary example of a meaningful democracy he really had to follow was that of the short-lived National Convention in France during the Jacobin period, which was the first government in the world to organise itself along the lines of universal male suffrage. Yet tragically, while the Parisian masses had been able to exert tremendous influence over the French Republic from 1793–94, there were strict material limits on what was possible for them to achieve and the French Revolution itself soon stalled, degenerated and fell back into reaction and the rise of Bonaparte. Indeed, if Louverture ultimately failed, as James would write in 1938 in *The Black Jacobins*, 'it is for the same reason that the Russian socialist revolution failed, even after all its achievements – the defeat of the revolution in Europe'.[46]

Contemporary Representations

In the contemporary period, Toussaint Louverture continues to serve as an inspirational, increasingly iconic figure. Despite the revelations historians have made about aspects of his life previous eclipsed by processes of mythologisation, most notably those relating to his status as an owner of slaves in his own right, this biographical information has been understood in its wider context, and Louverture's credentials as leader and precursor have continued to inspire numerous artistic and literary representations. In part, these have revisited and refigured previous versions of this revolutionary life. The Guyanese playwright and poet John Agard is exemplary in this regard, taking Wordsworth's 1802 sonnet 'To Toussaint L'Ouverture', and recasting the poem as 'Toussaint L'Ouverture acknowledges Wordsworth's sonnet "To Toussaint L'Ouverture"'. Agard underlines the differences between poet and revolutionary, stressing the transatlantic reach of his influence whilst underlining at the same time the solidarity this engenders:

My tongue bridges Europe to Dahomey.
Yet how sweet is the smell of liberty
when human beings share a common garment.[47]

In evidence too is the inspirational presence of Louverture in other media. The long tradition of representing the Haitian revolutionary leader in the visual arts has been continued by major recent work by artists including Édouard Duval-Carrié, François Cauvin, Kimathi Donkor, Lubaina Himid, Ulrick Jean-Pierre and Charlot Lucien. Jean-Michel Basquiat also produced a portrait of Louverture in 1983, and these representations have extended into sculpture where a number of busts and statues – most recently in Quebec City in 2010 – have been devoted to him. Literature also continues to satisfy a public interest in Louverture, who featured most notably in US novelist Madison Smartt Bell's trilogy on the Revolution, *All Souls' Rising* (1995), *Master of the Crossroads* (2000) and *The Stone That the Builder Refused* (2004). In his novel *In Darkness* (2012), British writer Nick Lake wove episodes from Louverture's life into his account of a young victim of the 2010 earthquake, and amongst Haitian and Haitian diasporic authors also, such as Jean-Claude Fignolé, Jean Métellus and Fabienne Pasquet, he has also inspired several recent novels.

Louverture has also featured in comics, challenging the reduction of Haiti in much US popular culture to 'voodoo' and zombies, and complementing an earlier tradition, seen in educational publications such the 'Golden Treasury' series, of turning the revolutionary leader into an inspiration for African-American young people. One of the most striking recent examples is *Drums of Freedom: The Saga of the Haitian Revolution*, by the Guyanese writer and illustrator Barrington

Braithwaite.[48] Based on careful consultation of the rich historiography of the struggle for Haitian independence, it draws in particular on C.L.R. James's *Black Jacobins*, as is the case with a number of contemporary representations. In music, too, artists such as Santana and the Calypsonian David M. Rudder have taken him as the subjects of their work, and this has been supplemented more recently by the Haitian rapper Wyclef Jean, who in part dedicated his album 'From the Hut, To the Projects, To the Mansion' to exploring the life of Louverture and his posthumous influence. The British rapper and poet Akala also includes the Haitian revolutionary – alongside Dessalines – in the hook of his song 'Malcolm Said It', where the lines: 'We love them dead when they speak no more / But they will endure, ideas are bulletproof' encapsulate the resilience of Louverture in the popular and political imagination.

Current representations continue to raise questions about the extent to which engagement with the leader of the Haitian Revolution domesticates Louverture's political implications for the present, or manages to retain elements of his incendiary force. Danny Glover intended for a number of years to produce a film of Louverture's life that promised to situate him in a frame of contemporary radicalism, but this has not yet appeared, meaning that the first major cinematic representation of the revolutionary was in a less politically engaged French mini-series of 2012, entitled *Toussaint Louverture*, in which the Haitian actor Jimmy Jean-Louis played the title role. Indeed the Haitian Revolution arguably still awaits its moment of cinematic glory. The film that has so far come closest to recognising the revolutionary spirit of the enslaved men, women and children who made the Haitian Revolution is *Quemada/Burn!* (1969), directed by the Italian socialist film-director Gillo Pontecorvo, best known for his anti-colonialist masterpiece, *The Battle of Algiers* (1966). The film, starring Marlon Brando, portrayed a failed slave revolt on a fictional colonial Caribbean island. It was a glorious fusion of Black Power, anti-Vietnam war sentiment, and hardened anti-imperialist politics – reflecting the impact of the current international explosion of struggles including those for independence in the Third World.

In a French context, Louverture has also been the subject of growing official recognition. His contribution to the abolition of slavery was marked in 1998, the year of the 150th anniversary of the second abolition in the French Empire (Louverture had, as we have seen, forced the first abolition during the Revolution in 1794), with an inscription in the French Pantheón that also acknowledged his death in detention in Joux; quotations from his speeches feature among the texts selected for the major memorial to abolitionism opened in Nantes in 2012. This official recognition tends, however, to continue to contribute to a tradition of conscription of Louverture to the French republican cause, downplaying his role in the revolutionary movements of the 1790s and refusing to acknowledge the ways in which the Revolution he led proposed forms of liberty, equality and fraternity largely unimagined and unimaginable in France itself.

This proliferation of representations of Louverture over the past decade reveals the ways in which his status as a revolutionary icon has acquired renewed intensity in a genuinely global frame.[49] Within these processes, there is nevertheless the risk that his specific implications in struggles for equality and liberation in the present may be diluted into generality. We need to consider closely the implications of the ubiquity of Louverture: he features as a character, for instance, in *Age of Empires III: The War Chiefs*, a real-time strategy game in which the Haitian revolutionary is available to serve the French or the British according to the player's whim; he features on t-shirts, hoodies and BBQ aprons; a Toussaint Louverture liqueur is now available (mix it with brandy to make a 'Napoléon noir' cocktail).

Such phenomena may suggest that any incendiary, revolutionary substance left in Louverture is being progressively eroded to be replaced by the ambivalence that characterises the few icons that we recognise as genuinely globalised. Che Guevara is the figure who most obviously fits this pattern, an icon of revolutionary struggle subject to neo-liberal recuperation through the mechanical reproduction of his image. The parallel is striking, for Louverture has long been the one revolutionary figure whose transnational visibility may be seen to rival that of Che. Both Haitian and Cuban float free from their actual revolutionary contexts, and risk in this process seeing a neutralisation of their historical, incendiary impact. Are we witnessing with Louverture a drift towards a commercialised global iconicity that elevates the Haitian revolutionary to rival Che, but at the same time sees him progressively emptied of his revolutionary, emancipatory meanings?

It is arguably in Haiti that, despite (or perhaps because of) continued debate about his legacy, Louverture retains his most potent force. In a country often divided between 'Louverturians' and 'Dessalineans', the man known as the 'Precursor' has long been central to the mechanisms adopted by his own country to embed the past in the present: in 2003, for instance, the international airport in Port-au-Prince was named after the revolutionary leader, and in the same year, the then president Jean-Bertrand Aristide used the bicentenary of Louverture's death to demand meticulously calculated reparations from France in compensation for the crippling debt paid by Haiti in return for recognition of its independence – over two decades after its declaration – in 1825.

The following year, despite his large popular mandate, Aristide was deposed by a coalition of Canadian, French and US forces and forced into African exile. On arrival at Bangui in the Central African Republic, he made a speech in which he claimed: 'Today, in the shadow of Toussaint Louverture, I declare: by overthrowing me, they have cut down the tree of peace, but this tree will grow up again because its roots are Louverturian.' He paraphrased Louverture's own words as he too had been forced to leave Haiti by the French occupying forces of Leclerc in 1802, reflecting the extent to which the revolutionary leader continues to symbolise not only resistance to external intervention in the country, but also the belief that an alternative future is possible. In capturing Louverture and condemning him to death in exile, Bonaparte sought to neutralise his rival and write him out of history. The First Consul had failed to understand, however, that the Haitian revolutionary had not only laid the foundations of an infrastructure of resistance and a national identity, but had also given form to a commitment to freedom that would not expire with him.

The persistent legacies of Louverture in contemporary Haiti are still apparent today as there is a search, post-earthquake, for those 'new narratives' that will permit continued engagement with the revolutionary past.[50] Nick Nesbitt has described Louverture as the architect of 'universal emancipation', and we are witnessing a re-grounding, an acknowledgement of the importance of Louverture as the figure who embodies the pushing of the American and French revolutions to unimaginable limits, the implications of which have not yet been fully realised. Louverture may still be seen, as a result, as an iconic reflection of historical resistance, as the leader of a revolution that outsmarted the colonial powers of Britain, France, Spain and the USA and delivered, one and half centuries before the age of mass decolonisation, an independent black republic in the Americas. He is also, however, an inspirational figure in contemporary struggles against injustice and oppression, associated not least with the ongoing resistance to economic and social persecution in contemporary Haiti itself.

We end with what remains the most famous homage to Louverture, the sonnet penned in August 1802 and published the following year by William Wordsworth, which reminds us why, as long as racism and imperialism persist as part of the modern world, Louverture will remain a revolutionary inspiration and icon. Racism arose alongside capitalism to legitimate and justify the Atlantic slave trade and the system of New World slavery at a time of growing 'Enlightenment', through perpetuating the idea that black people were inherently only fit to be, as the Bible had put it (Joshua 9: 23), 'hewers of wood and drawers of water'. As Paul Foot once noted of the *mental slavery* the planter class imposed and fostered among the enslaved in the Atlantic world:

> the whole operation survived on this notion . . . of the conquerable mind. That is that the minds of slaves, the minds of these black people from Africa were conquerable, that is they were to be conquered and conquerable all the way through. It wasn't only that there was savagery . . . it was also that they would never revolt. They could never revolt; it was not part of their makeup to do so.[51]

C.L.R. James, who as the author of not only *The Black Jacobins* but also in works such as *A History of Negro Revolt*, did more than almost any other historian to demonstrate that any idea the enslaved were ever 'docile' was a myth. As James noted in 1939, 'Negroes revolted against the slave raiders in Africa; they revolted against the slave traders on the Atlantic passage. They revolted on the plantations

. . . the only place where Negroes did not revolt is in the pages of capitalist historians.' Indeed, James declared that black revolutionary history was 'rich, inspiring and unknown', and there are few greater examples testifying to this than the Haitian Revolution itself, 'perhaps the most glorious victory of the oppressed over their oppressors in all history'.[52]

At one point in his biography of Louverture, Philippe Girard writes that 'he had many foes and no true friends'.[53] That Louverture, as a leader of 'the only successful slave revolt in history' had 'many foes' is not in doubt. As the Haitian revolutionary himself put it, 'Men who serve their country well . . . have powerful enemies . . . I know I shall perish a victim of calumny'.[54] This said, it was perhaps in response to the argument that he had 'no true friends' and seemed destined to 'perish a victim of calumny', which must have seemed self-evident to many contemporary observers in 1802 as Louverture was transported across the Atlantic to his lonely prison cell in Joux, that Wordsworth penned his tribute, 'To Toussaint Louverture':

> Live and take comfort, thou hast left behind
> Powers that will work for thee; air, earth and skies;
> There's not a breathing of the common wind
> That will forget thee; thou hast great allies;
> Thy friends are exultations, agonies
> And love, and man's unconquerable mind.

Notes

Introduction

1. René Depestre, 'An interview with Aimé Césaire', in Aimé Césaire, *Discourse on Colonialism* (New York: Monthly Review Press, 2000), p. 90. It should be noted that in this biography we follow Césaire in using the spelling 'Louverture' rather than 'L'Ouverture' throughout (except in direct quotes from other sources), as this is in keeping with how Louverture himself spelt his name after 1793.

2. Quoted in Philip Kaisary, *The Haitian Revolution in the Literary Imagination: Radical Horizons, Conservative Constraints* (Charlottesville: University of Virginia Press, 2014), pp. 26–7. For the full poem, see Aimé Césaire, *The Collected Poetry* (Berkeley: University of California Press, 1983), pp. 32–85. Kaisary also discusses Depestre's own tribute to the Haitian Revolution, *Un arc-en-ciel pour l'occident chrétien* [*A Rainbow for the Christian West*] (1967).

3. Kaisary, *The Haitian Revolution in the Literary Imagination*, p. 1.

4. In Haiti itself a rich nationalist historiography emerged from the mid-nineteenth century onwards, though only some of this has been translated into English. See, for example, Stephen Alexis, *Black Liberator: The Life of Toussaint Louverture*, trans. William Fernie Stirling (London: Ernest Benn, 1949). For a discussion, see Charles Forsdick, 'Toussaint Louverture and Haitian historiography: a pigmentocratic approach', in Chris Horrocks (ed.), *Cultures of Colour: Visual, Material, Textual* (Oxford: Berghahn, 2012), pp. 154–66.

5. Michel-Rolph Trouillot, *Silencing the Past: Power and the Production of History* (Boston: Beacon Press, 1995), p. 73.

6. Aimé Césaire, *Toussaint Louverture: La Révolution française et le problème colonial* (Paris: Présence Africaine, 1981).

7. See, for example, Peter Hallward, *Damming the Flood: Haiti, Aristide, and the Politics of Containment* (London: Verso, 2008).

8. For more discussion of C.L.R. James and his writing of *The Black Jacobins*, see Charles Forsdick and Christian Høgsbjerg (eds), *The Black Jacobins Reader* (Durham, NC: Duke University Press, 2017), and Christian Høgsbjerg, *C.L.R. James in Imperial Britain* (Durham, NC: Duke University Press, 2014).

9. James Walvin, 'Introduction' to C.L.R. James, *The Black Jacobins: Toussaint L'Ouverture and the Haitian Revolution* (London: Penguin, 2001), p. xiii. See Laurent Dubois, *Avengers of the New World: The Story of the Haitian Revolution* (Cambridge, MA: Harvard University Press, 2004).

10. C.L.R. James, *The Black Jacobins: Toussaint L'Ouverture and the Haitian Revolution* (London: Penguin, 2001), pp. xviii–xix.

11. Thomas Carlyle, *On Heroes, Hero-Worship and The Heroic in History* (London: Macmillan, 1917), pp. 1–2, 18.

12. For Carlyle on Louverture, see Alan Shelston (ed.), *Thomas Carlyle: Selected Writings* (Harmondsworth: Penguin, 1980), p. 195.

13. James, *The Black Jacobins*, pp. 73–4.

14. James, *The Black Jacobins*, p. 202.

15. This new methodology shaped the work of Carolyn Fick, one of James's students, in her study of the Haitian Revolution. See Carolyn Fick, *The Making of Haiti: The Saint-Domingue Revolution from Below* (Knoxville: University of Tennessee Press, 1997).

16. Percy Waxman, *The Black Napoleon: The Story of Toussaint Louverture* (New York: Harcourt, 1931), p. 5.

17. David Geggus, 'Underexploited sources', in *Haitian Revolutionary Studies* (Bloomington: Indiana University Press, 2002), pp. 43–51. See also Philippe Girard, 'The Haitian Revolution, History's New Frontier: State of the Scholarship and Archival Sources', *Slavery and Abolition*, 34, no. 3 (2013), pp. 485–507.

18. See Deborah Jenson, *Beyond the Slave Narrative: Politics, Sex and Manuscripts in the Haitian Revolution* (Liverpool: Liverpool University Press, 2011), pp. 45–80.

19. Philippe Girard and Jean-Louis Donnadieu, 'Toussaint before Louverture: New Archival Findings on the Early Life of Toussaint Louverture', *William and Mary Quarterly*, 70, no. 1 (2013), p. 77.

20. David A. Bell, 'Haiti's Jacobin', *The Nation*, 2 November 2016, www.thenation.com/article/haitis-jacobin/.

21. See Charles Forsdick, 'The travelling revolutionary: translations of Toussaint Louverture', in Martin Munro and Elizabeth Hackett-Walcott (eds), *Re-interpreting the Haitian Revolution and its Cultural Aftershocks* (St Augustine: UWI Press, 2006), pp. 150–67.

22. George F. Tyson (ed.), *Toussaint L'Ouverture* (Englewood Cliffs, NJ: Prentice-Hall, 1973), pp. 2–3.

23. Pierre Pluchon, *Toussaint Louverture: un révolutionnaire noir d'Ancien Régime* (Paris: Fayard, 1989).

24. C.A. Bayly, 'The Age of Revolutions in Global Context: An Afterword', in David Armitage and Sanjoy Subrahmanyam (eds), *The Age of Revolutions*

in *Global Context, c. 1760–1840* (Basingstoke: Palgrave Macmillan, 2010), p. 212.

25. See the dust jacket of Philippe Girard, *Toussaint Louverture: A Revolutionary Life* (New York: Basic Books, 2016).

26. Girard, *Toussaint Louverture*, pp. 4–5.

27. Girard, *Toussaint Louverture*, pp. 5, 82.

28. For an excellent discussion of the slave ship as among other things a factory, see Marcus Rediker, *The Slave Ship: A Human History* (London: John Murray, 2007).

29. When Selma James addressed the Aristide Foundation for Democracy in Haiti in 2011, she articulated the choice that still underpins the role of education in postcolonial societies: 'to rise out of poverty . . . or to work to eliminate poverty . . . for all of us to rise out of poverty together. Not leaving our community behind'. See Selma James, *Sex, Race and Class: The Perspective of Winning; A Selection of Writings 1952–2011* (Chicago: PM Press, 2012), p. 10.

30. James, *The Black Jacobins*, p. xix.

31. Girard, *Toussaint Louverture,* pp. 24, 28.

32. Girard, *Toussaint Louverture*, p. 193.

33. James, *The Black Jacobins*, p. 211.

34. Quoted in David Armitage and Sanjoy Subrahmanyam, 'Introduction: The Age of Revolutions, c.1760–1840 – Global Causation, Connection, and Comparison', in David Armitage and Sanjoy Subrahmanyam (eds), *The Age of Revolutions in Global Context, c. 1760–1840* (Basingstoke: Palgrave Macmillan, 2010), p. xiii.

35. Armitage and Subrahmanyam, 'Introduction: The Age of Revolutions, c.1760–1840 – Global Causation, Connection, and Comparison', in *The Age of Revolutions in Global Context*, p. xvii.

36. Lynn Hunt 'The French Revolution in Global Context' in Armitage and Subrahmanyam, *The Age of Revolutions in Global Context*, p. 23. Hunt also notes that 'Simon Schama gives one sentence in his 950 pages of *Citizens* (1989) to the slave uprising of 1791, and then only to explain the high price of sugar in Paris in 1792'. Godechot devoted merely half a page to the Haitian Revolution in his work. See Jacques Godechot, *France and the Atlantic Revolution of the Eighteenth Century, 1770–1799* (New York: The Free Press, 1971), p. 230.

37. Eric J. Hobsbawm, *The Age of Revolution: Europe 1789–1848* (London: Cardinal, 1988), pp. 14–16, 91, 389.

38. Richard Cobb, *The French and their Revolution* (London: John Murray, 1998), p. 35.

39. Armitage and Subrahmanyam, 'Introduction: The Age of Revolutions, c.1760–1840 – Global Causation, Connection, and Comparison', p. xiii.

For Armitage and Subrahmanyam, the 'Age of Revolutions' for some reason closes not with the wave of revolutions across Europe in 1848 but with the start of Anglo-Chinese Opium War (1839–42).

Chapter 1: Toussaint Unchained: c. 1743–91

1. Quoted in Wenda Parkinson, *'This Gilded African': Toussaint L'Ouverture* (London: Quartet Books, 1978), p. 37.
2. Philippe Girard, *Paradise Lost: Haiti's Tumultuous Journey from Pearl of the Caribbean to Third World Hot Spot* (Houndmills, New York: Palgrave Macmillan, 2005).
3. For more precise estimates, see Jeremy Popkin, *A Concise History of the Haitian Revolution* (Chichester: Wiley-Blackwell, 2011), p. 12.
4. James, *The Black Jacobins*, p. 9.
5. James, *The Black Jacobins*, p. 8.
6. Ralph Korngold, *Citizen Toussaint* (London: Victor Gollancz, 1945), p. 258.
7. Girard, *Toussaint Louverture*, p. 8.
8. Girard, *Toussaint Louverture*, p. 17.
9. Madison Smartt Bell, *Toussaint Louverture: A Biography* (New York: Vintage Books, 2008), p. 61.
10. Girard, *Toussaint Louverture*, p. 19.
11. Girard, *Toussaint Louverture*, p. 22.
12. Cited in Laurent Dubois and John D. Garrigus, *Slave Revolution in the Caribbean, 1789–1804: A Brief History with Documents* (Boston; Bedford: St Martins, 2006), p. 56.
13. James, *The Black Jacobins*, p. 74.
14. James, *The Black Jacobins*, p. 74.
15. Bell, *Toussaint Louverture*, p. 19.
16. Girard, *Toussaint Louverture*, p. 31.
17. Girard, *Toussaint Louverture*, p. 101.
18. Girard, *Toussaint Louverture*, p. 44.
19. Caffarelli's report to Bonaparte is included in Toussaint-Louverture, *Mémoires, suivi du journal du général Caffarelli* (Paris: Mercure de France, 2016), pp. 109–32.
20. Gabriel Debien, Jean Fouchard and Marie Antoinette Menier, 'Toussaint Louverture avant 1789: légendes et réalités', *Conjonction: revue franco-haitienne*, 134 (1977), 66–80. In a letter of 1797, Louverture comments that he had by that time been free for 20 years. Cited by Girard and Donnadieu, 'Toussaint before Louverture', p. 67.
21. Girard, *Toussaint Louverture*, p. 53.
22. Girard, *Toussaint Louverture*, pp. 54–5.

23. Girard and Donnadieu, 'Toussaint before Louverture', p. 70. According to Girard, it came to light in 2012 that one of Toussaint's slaves was none other than Jean-Jacques Dessalines, who later became the first leader of independent Haiti, which certainly casts new light on the relationship between these two leading revolutionaries. Girard, *Toussaint Louverture*, pp. 72–3.

24. Girard, *Toussaint Louverture*, p. 51.

25. Vladimir I. Lenin, *Left-Wing Communism: An Infantile Disorder* (London: Bookmarks, 1993), p. 118.

26. Dubois, *Avengers of the New World*, pp. 30, 35.

27. Girard, *Toussaint Louverture*, p. 96.

28. Lenin, *Left-Wing Communism*, p. 118.

29. Dubois, *Avengers of the New World*, p. 30.

30. Girard, *Toussaint Louverture*, p. 71.

31. Cited in Dubois and Garrigus, *Slave Revolution in the Caribbean, 1789–1804*, p. 76.

32. Dubois, *Avengers of the New World*, p. 88.

33. Girard, *Toussaint Louverture*, p. 103.

34. Lenin, *Left-Wing Communism*, p. 118.

35. Dubois, *Avengers of the New World*, pp. 30, 59.

36. Thomas Carlyle, *The French Revolution: A History*, Vol. II (London: Chapman & Hall, 1837), p. 186.

37. Explored in Fick, *The Making of Haiti*.

38. James, *The Black Jacobins*, p. 66.

39. Girard, *Toussaint Louverture*, pp. 107–8.

40. James, *The Black Jacobins*, p. 73.

Chapter 2: Making an Opening to Liberty: 1791–93

1. David Patrick Geggus, *Haitian Revolutionary Studies* (Bloomington: Indiana University Press, 2002), p. 88. Dutty was known as 'Zamba' from *nzamba*, or 'elephant' because of his size, by his Kongolose followers. See John K. Thornton, '"I Am the Subject of the King of Congo": African Political Ideology and the Haitian Revolution', *Journal of World History*, 4, 2 (1993), p. 185.

2. See the earliest account of the Bois Caïman ceremony written in 1793 by the doctor Antoine Dalmas who used an interrogation of participants who tried to kill one of the plantation managers on the Galliffet estate the next morning in David Geggus (ed.), *The Haitian Revolution: A Documentary History* (Indianapolis: Hackett, 2014), pp. 78–9. See also the 1824 account by the Haitian politician Hérard Dumesle in his Voyage to the north of Haiti, reproduced in Laurent Dubois and John D. Garrigus, *Slave Revolution*

in the Caribbean, 1789–1804, pp. 86–8. On Cécile Fatiman, see Joan Dayan, *Haiti, History and the Gods* (Berkeley: University of California Press, 1998), p. 47.

3. James, *The Black Jacobins*, pp. 70–1.

4. Laurent Dubois, *Avengers of the New World*, pp. 102, 105.

5. Dubois, *Avengers of the New World*, p. 89.

6. Fick, *The Making of* Haiti, pp. 105–6. For an excellent detailed account of the August insurrection, see *The Making of Haiti*, pp. 102–12.

7. Geggus (ed.), *The Haitian Revolution*, p. 92.

8. Bell, *Toussaint Louverture*, pp. 78–9.

9. Bell, *Toussaint Louverture*, p. 87.

10. Girard, *Toussaint Louverture*, pp. 109–10.

11. Geggus, *Haitian Revolutionary Studies*, pp. 84–5. See also the report of the Lenormand meeting in Geggus (ed.), *The Haitian Revolution*, pp. 77–8.

12. Fick, *The Making of Haiti*, p. 92.

13. Quoted in James, *The Black Jacobins*, pp. 70–1. See also Geggus, *Haitian Revolutionary Studies*, p. 89.

14. Bell, *Toussaint Louverture*, pp. 81–2.

15. James, *The Black Jacobins*, p. 73.

16. Girard, *Toussaint Louverture*, p. 111.

17. Girard, *Toussaint Louverture*, p. 111.

18. Bell, *Toussaint Louverture*, pp. 82–3.

19. Girard, *Toussaint Louverture*, p. 115.

20. Bell, *Toussaint Louverture*, p. 81.

21. Bell, *Toussaint Louverture*, p. 33.

22. Dubois, *Avengers of the New World*, p. 98. See also Geggus (ed.), *The Haitian Revolution*, p. 78.

23. Dubois, *Avengers of the New World*, p. 109. For more on this, see Thornton, '"I Am the Subject of the King of Congo"', pp. 187–8.

24. Dubois, *Avengers of the New World*, p. 124. For an account of Boukman Dutty's humanitarianism amidst the insurrection, see Jeremy D. Popkin, *Facing Racial Revolution: Eyewitness Accounts of the Haitian Insurrection* (Chicago: University of Chicago Press, 2008), pp. 49–58. As Blackburn notes, the officer who reported Boukman Dutty's death 'noted the presence of five cannon and a white man with Boukman's force of several hundred'. Robin Blackburn, *The Overthrow of Colonial Slavery 1776–1848* (London: Verso, 1996), p. 192.

25. Dubois, *Avengers of the New World*, p. 106.

26. Quoted in Nick Nesbitt, *Universal Emancipation: The Haitian Revolution and the Radical Enlightenment* (Charlottesville: University of Virginia Press, 2008), p. 143.

27. Jane Landers suggests that the friendship of Biassou and Louverture had been forged through their connections to the Fathers of Charity in Cap Français, a religious organisation on whose sugar plantation Biassou is thought to have been a *commandeur*. Biassou's correspondence contains references to his Catholic faith, suggesting a clear indebtedness to this group for his own education. See Jane G. Landers, *Atlantic Creoles in the Age of Revolutions* (Cambridge, MA: Harvard University Press, 2010), p. 58, and Bell, *Toussaint Louverture*, p. 64.

28. Dubois, *Avengers of the New World*, p. 109.

29. For more on West African military organisation in the New World, see Manuel Barcia, *West African Warfare in Bahia and Cuba: Soldier Slaves in the Atlantic World, 1807–1844* (Oxford: Oxford University Press, 2014).

30. John R. Beard, *The Life of Toussaint L'Ouverture* (Seattle: Inkling, 2002), p. 38. This letter is also reproduced with a slightly different translation in Geggus (ed.), *The Haitian Revolution*, pp. 82–3.

31. Beard, *The Life of Toussaint L'Ouverture*, p. 38. The uncompromising tone here perhaps owed something to the fact that Jeannot Billet had a part in writing this letter. See David Geggus, 'Print Culture and the Haitian Revolution: The Written and the Spoken Word', in David S. Shields and Mariselle Meléndez (eds), *Liberty! Égalité! Independencia!: Print Culture, Enlightenment, and Revolution in the Americas, 1776–1838* (Worcester, MA: American Antiquarian Society, 2007), p. 89.

32. Bell, *Toussaint Louverture*, pp. 23–4, 33.

33. Toussaint Louverture, 'Letter to Biassou' in Nick Nesbitt (ed.), *Toussaint Louverture: The Haitian Revolution*, pp. 3–4. On Biassou and Bréda before the revolution, see Girard, *Toussaint Louverture*, p. 58.

34. James, *The Black Jacobins*, p. 84.

35. For the text of this letter, see Dubois and Garrigus, *Slave Revolution in the Caribbean*, pp. 100–11.

36. Dubois and Garrigus, *Slave Revolution in the Caribbean*, p. 111. Blackburn has suggested that this was not a 'betrayal' by the leaders despite their 'egotism and condescension', as given 'the uneven and incomplete development of slave resistance and revolt', though 'elite slaves already enjoyed privileges and aspired to full freedom; the mass of slaves might be willing to settle for improved conditions . . . and could be satisfied by promises of more time to work their plots.' See Blackburn, *The Overthrow of Colonial Slavery*, p. 194.

37. Quoted in Deborah Jenson, *Beyond the Slave Narrative: Politics, Sex, and Manuscripts in the Haitian Revolution* (Liverpool: Liverpool University Press, 2011), pp. 53–4.

38. James, *The Black Jacobins*, p. 86. See also Geggus (ed.), *The Haitian Revolution*, pp. 73, 83–5, and Nesbitt, *Universal Emancipation*, p. 143.

39. James, *The Black Jacobins*, pp. 87–8. Again, also see Geggus (ed.), *The Haitian Revolution*, pp. 73, 87–9.

40. David Geggus, 'Toussaint Louverture and the Haitian Revolution', in *Profiles of Revolutionaries in Atlantic History, 1750–1850*, ed. R.W. Weisberger, D.P. Hupchick, D.L. Anderson (New York: Columbia University Press, 2007), pp. 119–21. James, *The Black Jacobins*, p. 88.

41. Girard, *Toussaint Louverture*, p. 124.

42. James, *The Black Jacobins*, pp. 95–6; Bell, *Toussaint Louverture*, p. 43.

43. Geggus, 'Print Culture and the Haitian Revolution', p. 89.

44. Nesbitt (ed.), *Toussaint Louverture*, p. 6.

45. Nesbitt (ed.), *Toussaint Louverture*, pp. 6–7.

46. Nesbitt (ed.) *Toussaint Louverture*, p. 7.

47. Nesbitt (ed.) *Toussaint Louverture*, pp. 7–8.

48. Girard, *Toussaint Louverture*, p. 125.

49. James, *The Black Jacobins*, p. 101.

50. James, *The Black Jacobins*, p. 99.

51. James, *The Black Jacobins*, p. 101.

52. Dubois, *Avengers of the New World*, p. 153. In mid-1793, Jean-François alone claimed to command 6,647 men. See David Geggus, 'The Arming of Slaves in the Haitian Revolution', in Christopher Leslie Brown and Philip D. Morgan (eds), *Arming Slaves: From Classical Times to the Modern Age* (New Haven: Yale University Press, 2006), p. 222. On the French reinforcements, see Girard, *Toussaint Louverture*, p. 131.

53. James, *The Black Jacobins*, p. 101. See also Dubois, *Avengers of the New World*, p. 177.

54. Bell, *Toussaint Louverture*, pp. 45–6.

55. Nesbitt, *Universal Emancipation*, p. 147.

56. Bell, *Toussaint Louverture*, p. 53.

57. Jeremy D. Popkin, *You Are All Free: The Haitian Revolution and the Abolition of Slavery* (Cambridge: Cambridge University Press, 2010), p. 2.

58. Bell, *Toussaint Louverture*, p. 54. See also Geggus (ed.), *The Haitian Revolution*, p. 122.

59. Popkin, *You Are All Free*, p. 10.

60. Hunt, 'The French Revolution in Global Context', p. 27.

61. Nesbitt, *Universal Emancipation*, pp. 145–6.

62. Geggus (ed.), *The Haitian Revolution*, p. 124.

63. Nesbitt, *Universal Emancipation*, p. 146.

64. Geggus (ed.), *The Haitian Revolution*, p. 123.

65. Dubois and Garrigus, *Slave Revolution in the Caribbean*, p. 128.

66. Dubois, *Avengers of the New World*, pp. 163, 165. See also Geggus (ed.), *The Haitian Revolution*, p. 99.

67. Geggus (ed.), *The Haitian Revolution*, pp. 108–9.

68. Robert Louis Stein, *Léger Félicité Sonthonax* (Cranbury, NJ: Associated University Presses, 1985), p. 89. For the full text of the emancipation proclamation, see Geggus (ed.), *The Haitian Revolution*, pp. 107–9.

69. The other commissioner Polverel would follow Sonthonax with similar edicts in the South and West Provinces in October 1793. See Popkin, *You Are All Free*, p. 278. See also Geggus (ed.), *The Haitian Revolution*, pp. 99, 102.

70. Geggus (ed.), *The Haitian Revolution*, p. 111.

71. Dubois, *Avengers of the New World*, p. 177.

72. Geggus (ed.), *The Haitian Revolution*, pp. 125–6.

73. Dubois, *Avengers of the New World*, p. 159. See also the account of the camp of Biassou and Jean-François by a Spanish officer in August 1793, in Geggus (ed.) *The Haitian Revolution*, pp. 110–11.

74. Bell, *Toussaint Louverture*, p. 55.

75. Dubois and Garrigus, *Slave Revolution in the Caribbean*, p. 127.

76. Dubois and Garrigus, *Slave Revolution in the Caribbean*, p. 126.

77. Quoted in Jenson, *Beyond the Slave Narrative*, p. 48.

78. Ralph Korngold, *Citizen Toussaint*, p. 85. See also Dubois, *Avengers of the New World*, p. 172.

79. Korngold, *Citizen Toussaint*, p. 86.

80. Bell, *Toussaint Louverture*, p. 56.

81. Geggus (ed.), *The Haitian Revolution*, p. 123. For an example of Sonthonax's view of liberty as something that is imposed from above, see his letter to Louverture in early 1794 noting that since his proclamation of 29 August 1793, 'France has authorised us to declare you free'. Quoted in Nesbitt, *Universal Emancipation*, pp. 147–8.

82. Korngold, *Citizen Toussaint*, p. 86.

Chapter 3: Black Jacobin Ascending: 1793–98

1. Roger Norman Buckley, 'Introduction' to *The Haitian Journal of Lieutenant Howard, York Hussars, 1796–1798* (Knoxville: University of Tennessee Press, 1985), p. xxi.

2. Buckley, 'Introduction', pp. xxiv–xxv, and Dubois, *Avengers of the New World*, p. 166.

3. Geggus (ed.), *The Haitian Revolution*, p. 112.

4. Dubois, *Avengers of the New World*, p. 169; James, *The Black Jacobins*, p. 113. For the transcript of the debate, see Dubois and Garrigus, *Slave Revolution in the Caribbean*, pp. 129–32.

5. James, *The Black Jacobins*, pp. 113–14.

6. Dubois, *Avengers of the New World*, p. 170. For the text of the decree, see Geggus (ed.), *The Haitian Revolution*, p. 112.

7. Blackburn, *The Overthrow of Colonial Slavery*, p. 225.
8. Buckley, 'Introduction', p. xxv.
9. Geggus, *Haitian Revolutionary Studies*, p. 130.
10. Buckley, 'Introduction', p. xxvi.
11. Bryan Edwards, quoted in David Geggus, *Slavery, War, and Revolution: The British Occupation of Saint Domingue, 1793–1798* (Oxford: Oxford University Press, 1982), p. 121.
12. Geggus, *Haitian Revolutionary Studies*, p. 131. Dubois, *Avengers of the New World*, p. 168. On *La Légion de l'Égalité*, see Geggus, 'The Arming of Slaves in the Haitian Revolution', p. 223.
13. Stein, *Léger Félicité Sonthonax*, p. 100.
14. Stein, *Léger Félicité Sonthonax*, p. 101.
15. Geggus, *Haitian Revolutionary Studies*, p. 131.
16. Geggus, *Haitian Revolutionary Studies*, pp. 129, 131. See also Louverture's letters to the Governor of Santo Domingo in March 1794 attacking Biassou as among other things 'a simple, vulnerable man without much knowledge . . . easily led astray by the scoundrels surrounding him'. Geggus (ed.), *The Haitian Revolution*, p. 127.
17. Geggus, *Haitian Revolutionary Studies*, p. 133.
18. Geggus, *Haitian Revolutionary Studies*, p. 133.
19. Dubois, *Avengers of the New World*, p. 179. See also Korngold, *Citizen Toussaint*, p. 86.
20. Toussaint Louverture, 'Letter to General Laveaux', in Nesbitt (ed.), *Toussaint Louverture*, p. 9.
21. Louverture, 'Letter to General Laveaux', p. 10.
22. Blackburn, *The Overthrow of Colonial Slavery*, p. 221.
23. Stein, *Léger Félicité Sonthonax*, p. 104.
24. Geggus, 'Toussaint Louverture and the Haitian Revolution', pp. 123–4.
25. Louverture, 'Letter to General Laveaux', p. 10.
26. Toussaint Louverture, 'Letter to Laveaux', in Nesbitt (ed.), *Toussaint Louverture*, pp. 11–12.
27. Louverture, 'Letter to Laveaux', p. 12.
28. Dubois, *Avengers of the New World*, p. 180.
29. Dubois, *Avengers of the New World*, p. 182. For the size of Jean-François's army in late 1794, see Geggus, 'The Arming of Slaves in the Haitian Revolution', p. 222.
30. Geggus, *Slavery, War and Revolution*, pp. 131–2.
31. Dubois, *Avengers of the New World*, p. 182. For the size of Jean-François's army in mid-1793 and February 1795, see Geggus, 'The Arming of Slaves in the Haitian Revolution', p. 222.
32. Toussaint Louverture, 'Letter to Jean-François', in Nesbitt (ed.), *Toussaint Louverture*, p. 16.

33. James, *The Black Jacobins*, pp. 128–9.
34. Geggus, 'Print Culture and the Haitian Revolution', p. 92.
35. Dubois, *Avengers of the New World*, p. 183.
36. Geggus, *Slavery, War and Revolution*, pp. 128–9.
37. Dubois, *Avengers of the New World*, p. 181.
38. Korngold, *Citizen Toussaint*, pp. 86–7.
39. As Dubois notes, 'the British, worried about the precedent that might otherwise be set for their own colonies, decided in mid-1793 to apply discriminatory British law in Saint-Domingue', reintroducing a colour bar for the police and administrative posts. Dubois, *Avengers of the New World*, p. 181.
40. Buckley, 'Introduction', pp. xxviii–xxix.
41. Dubois and Garrigus, *Slave Revolution in the Caribbean*, p. 147.
42. David Brion Davis, *Inhuman Bondage: The Rise and Fall of Slavery in the New World* (Oxford: Oxford University Press, 2006), p. 166.
43. James, *The Black Jacobins*, p. 109. Given the actual and potential riches that were threatened by slave resistance and revolt, this was a misleading statement, and as C.L.R. James commented, 'Dundas knew that not a single member of Parliament would believe him. But Parliament has always agreed to speak in these terms in order to keep the people quiet.'
44. Buckley, 'Introduction', pp. xxxi–xxxiii, xliii.
45. Dubois, *Avengers of the New World*, pp. 183–4.
46. Geggus, *Slavery, War and Revolution*, p. 388. On the British Chasseurs, see Geggus, 'The Arming of Slaves in the Haitian Revolution, pp. 225–6.
47. Toussaint Louverture, 'Letter to Dieudonné' in Nesbitt (ed.) *Toussaint Louverture*, pp. 18–20.
48. Dubois, *Avengers of the New World*, p. 199.
49. Buckley, 'Introduction', p. li. Roger Norman Buckley (ed.), *The Haitian Journal of Lieutenant Howard, York Hussars, 1796–1798* (Knoxville: University of Tennessee Press, 1985), p. 134.
50. Buckley (ed.), *The Haitian Journal of Lieutenant Howard*, pp. 49–50.
51. Buckley (ed.), *The Haitian Journal of Lieutenant Howard*, pp. 53–4.
52. Korngold, *Citizen Toussaint*, p. 92.
53. Buckley, 'Introduction', p. xxxv.
54. Bell, *Toussaint Louverture*, pp. 133–4. See also the letters from Louverture to Laveaux in April 1796, in Geggus (ed.), *The Haitian Revolution*, pp. 128–9.
55. Quoted in Jenson, *Beyond the Slave Narrative*, p. 69.
56. Geggus, 'Toussaint Louverture and the Haitian Revolution', pp. 125–6.
57. Toussaint Louverture, 'Letter to Laveaux', in Nesbitt (ed.), *Toussaint Louverture*, p. 30. See also Dubois, *Avengers of the New World*, p. 215.
58. Geggus, *Slavery, War and Revolution*, p. 200.

59. Korngold, *Citizen Toussaint*, p. 92.

60. Buckley (ed.) *The Haitian Journal of Lieutenant Howard*, p. 177, n.134.

61. Buckley (ed.) *The Haitian Journal of Lieutenant Howard*, pp. 91–2.

62. Buckley (ed.) *The Haitian Journal of Lieutenant Howard*, p. 93.

63. Dubois, *Avengers of the New World*, p. 215. See also Geggus, *Slavery, War and Revolution*, p. 224.

64. Marcus Rainsford, *An Historical Account of the Black Empire of Hayti* (Durham, NC: Duke University Press, 2013), pp. 134–5.

65. Korngold, *Citizen Toussaint*, p. 119. See also James, *The Black Jacobins*, p. 164.

66. Geggus, *Slavery, War, and Revolution*, pp. 362, 382. Geggus estimates the overall cost of Pitt's campaigns across the West Indies in this period to be about 35,000 soldiers dead at the cost of £20 million. See David Geggus, 'The Cost of Pitt's Caribbean Campaigns, 1793–1798', *The Historical Journal*, 26, no. 3 (1983), 699–706. It is impossible to estimate precisely what this might be equivalent to today, but for reference Britain's GDP in the period 1791–1800 has been estimated as being about £135 million (at 1851–60 prices). See C.H. Feinstein, 'Capital Formation in Great Britain', in Peter Mathias and M.M. Postan (eds), *The Cambridge Economic History of Europe*, Vol. VII, Part I (Cambridge: Cambridge University Press, 1978), p. 91. This might mean the Saint-Domingue campaign was perhaps comparative to about 5 per cent of UK GDP, and Pitt's Caribbean campaign as a whole perhaps 15 per cent of UK GDP.

67. Geggus, *Slavery, War and Revolution*, pp. 212, 275.

68. Dubois, *Avengers of the New World*, pp. 216–18. As Geggus notes, the British occupation of Saint-Domingue was deemed 'an episode best forgotten' in British history, though in Sacred Trinity Church on Chapel Street in Salford, Lancashire a funeral monument to Major Thomas Drinkwater has an inscription to his past role in Saint-Domingue: 'Thrice had his foot Domingo's island prest, Midst horrid wars and fierce barbarian wiles; Thrice had his blood repelled the yellow pest That stalks, gigantic, through the Western Isles!' Geggus, *Slavery, War and Revolution*, pp. 387–8.

69. Michael Duffy, 'World-Wide War and British Expansion, 1793–1815', in P.J. Marshall (ed.), *The Oxford History of the British Empire: The Eighteenth Century* (Oxford: Oxford University Press, 1998), pp. 195–6. The British Empire would also be rocked by rebellion in Ireland in 1798 led by the United Irishmen.

70. Michel Rolph-Trouillot, *Silencing the Past*, p. 89.

71. Bell, *Toussaint Louverture*, pp. 150–4. Sonthonax now bitterly denounced Toussaint as a royalist reactionary, claiming 'at the instigation of those same émigrés that surround him today, he organised in 1791 the revolt of the Blacks and the massacre of the landowning Whites. In 1793 he

commanded the army of brigands at the orders of the Catholic king.' See also the account of the clash between Sonthonax and Louverture written by the commissioner Julien Raimond (a rival of Sonthonax), which has Louverture accusing Sonthonax of trying to trick him into pushing for independence from France, in Geggus (ed.), *The Haitian Revolution*, pp. 135–8. This is discussed in Jenson, *Beyond the Slave Narrative*, pp. 70–3.

72. Geggus, 'Toussaint Louverture and the Haitian Revolution', pp. 125–6. Bell, *Toussaint Louverture*, pp. 163–5.

73. Bell, *Toussaint Louverture*, p. 165.

74. James, *The Black Jacobins*, p. 180. Some of those who refused to tremble before Louverture, even if former black insurgent leaders like Pierre-Michel, Thomas Mondion and Barthélemy were arrested and executed. See Geggus (ed.), *The Haitian Revolution*, p. 140.

75. Geggus, *Slavery, War and Revolution*, p. 390.

76. Dubois, *Avengers of the New World*, p. 215.

77. Dubois and Garrigus, *Slave Revolution in the Caribbean*, pp. 157–8.

78. Quoted in David Geggus, 'British Opinion and the Emergence of Haiti, 1791–1805', in James Walvin (ed), *Slavery and British Society 1776–1846* (London: Macmillan, 1982), p. 130.

79. James, *The Black Jacobins*, pp. 197–8.

80. James, *The Black Jacobins*, p. 215.

81. James, *The Black Jacobins*, p. 120. That African ideas of kingship, which were often far more contradictory and complex than they might at first appear, were ever fully 'transcended' during the Haitian Revolution is unlikely. See Thornton, '"I Am the Subject of the King of Congo"'.

82. Toussaint Louverture, 'Address to soldiers for the universal destruction of slavery', in Nesbitt (ed.), *Toussaint Louverture*, p. 28.

83. Louverture, 'Letter to Laveaux', p. 31.

84. Toussaint Louverture, 'Letter to the Directory, 28 October 1797', in Tyson (ed.), *Toussaint Louverture*, pp. 40–2. This letter is reproduced in Geggus (ed.), *The Haitian Revolution*, pp. 143–5, and also Dubois and Garrigus, *Slave Revolution in the Caribbean*, pp. 148–53.

85. Toussaint Louverture, 'Letter to the French Directory', in Nesbitt (ed.) *Toussaint Louverture*, pp. 34–5.

86. James, *The Black Jacobins*, pp. 161–2.

Chapter 4: The Black Robespierre: 1798–1801

1. James, *The Black Jacobins*, pp. 180–1.

2. For Laveaux's 1798 speech, see Dubois and Garrigus, *Slave Revolution in the Caribbean*, pp. 156–8. How much Louverture knew about the 'Second Maroon War' in Jamaica from 1795–96 is unclear, but on this see, Michael

Craton, *Testing the Chains: Resistance to Slavery in the British West Indies* (Ithaca: Cornell University Press, 1982), pp. 211–23.

3. Dubois, *Avengers of the New World*, pp. 219, 223.

4. Dubois, *Avengers of the New World*, pp. 223, 225. James, *The Black Jacobins*, p. 184.

5. Dubois, *Avengers of the New World*, pp. 223–4. See also Gordon S. Brown, *Toussaint's Clause: The Founding Fathers and the Haitian Revolution* (Jackson: University Press of Mississippi, 2005), and Ronald Angelo Johnson, *Diplomacy in Black and White: John Adams, Toussaint Louverture, and their Atlantic World Alliance* (Athens; London: University of Georgia Press, 2014).

6. Girard, *Toussaint Louverture*, p. 184. See also Bell, *Toussaint Louverture*, p. 183, and Dubois, *Avengers of the New World*, p. 225.

7. Dubois, *Avengers of the New World*, p. 231.

8. James, *The Black Jacobins*, p. 182.

9. James, *The Black Jacobins*, p. 183.

10. During the war, Bauvais relinquished his command and left the colony with the aim of sailing to France, but he drowned *en voyage*. James, *The Black Jacobins*, p. 188. Dubois, *Avengers of the New World*, pp. 235–6.

11. Dubois, *Avengers of the New World*, pp. 232–4.

12. Dubois, *Avengers of the New World*, p. 233. See also the contemporary account of Pélage-Marie Duboys, a white lawyer based in Port-au-Prince about the respective arguments of Rigaud and Louverture in this period, republished in Geggus (ed.), *The Haitian Revolution*, pp. 148–51.

13. Dubois, *Avengers of the New World*, p. 234.

14. Nesbitt, *Universal Emancipation*, p. 204.

15. Korngold, *Citizen Toussaint*, p. 147.

16. 'Bonaparte's Letter to St-Domingue', in Nesbitt (ed.), *Toussaint Louverture*, p. 37. For the Directory's 1798 'Law on the Colonies', see Dubois and Garrigus, *Slave Revolution in the Caribbean*, pp. 153–5.

17. Dubois, *Avengers of the New World*, p. 236.

18. James, *The Black Jacobins*, p. 228.

19. Dubois, *Avengers of the New World*, p. 193.

20. Dubois, *Avengers of the New World*, pp. 227, 230.

21. Dubois, *Avengers of the New World*, p. 185. 'The problem of freedom' was a phrase coined by one historian of slavery in Jamaica, Thomas C. Holt. See Thomas Holt, *The Problem of Freedom: Race, Labor, and Politics in Jamaica and Britain, 1832–1938* (Baltimore, MD: Johns Hopkins University Press, 1991).

22. Dubois and Garrigus, *Slave Revolution in the Caribbean*, pp. 140, 142.

23. Dubois and Garrigus, *Slave Revolution in the Caribbean*, p. 142.

24. Dubois, *Avengers of the New World*, pp. 186–7.

25. Dubois and Garrigus, *Slave Revolution in the Caribbean*, p. 143.

26. 'Toussaint L'Ouverture to his brothers and sisters in Varettes', in Nesbitt (ed.), *Toussaint Louverture: The Haitian Revolution*, p. 15.

27. Dubois, *Avengers of the New World*, p. 189.

28. Toussaint Louverture, 'Letter to Laveaux', in Nesbitt (ed.), *Toussaint Louverture: The Haitian Revolution*, pp. 21–2. This letter is also in Geggus (ed.), *The Haitian Revolution*, pp. 129–31.

29. Louverture, 'Letter to Laveaux', p. 22.

30. Louverture, 'Letter to Laveaux', p. 23. Datty would later be executed in September 1796 after further rebellions. See Geggus (ed.) *The Haitian Revolution*, p. 129.

31. Louverture, 'Letter to Laveaux', p. 24.

32. Geggus (ed.), *The Haitian Revolution*, p. 131.

33. Geggus (ed.), *The Haitian Revolution*, p. 131.

34. James, *The Black Jacobins*, p. 201.

35. See the extract from Rainsford's *An Historical Account of the Black Empire of Hayti* (1805) reproduced in Geggus (ed.), *The Haitian Revolution*, pp. 155–6.

36. Bell, *Toussaint Louverture*, p. 168.

37. Dubois, *Avengers of the New World*, p. 244. Bell, *Toussaint Louverture*, pp. 194–6.

38. Toussaint Louverture, 'Proclamation on Labour', in Nesbitt (ed.), *Toussaint Louverture*, pp. 38–9. See also George F. Tyson (ed.), *Toussaint L'Ouverture*, pp. 51–6, and Geggus (ed.), *The Haitian Revolution*, pp. 153–4.

39. Fick, *The Making of Haiti*, p. 208. For detailed descriptions of the inevitably rather chaotic state of two plantations on the southeast coast in August 1798, see Geggus (ed.), *The Haitian Revolution*, pp. 151–3.

40. Dubois, *Avengers of the New World*, pp. 239–40.

41. Dubois, *Avengers of the New World*, p. 240. See also Christopher Hill, *Liberty Against the Law: Some Seventeenth-century Controversies* (London: Penguin, 1997).

42. Fick, *The Making of Haiti*, p. 208.

43. Geggus, 'Toussaint Louverture and the Haitian Revolution', pp. 129–30.

44. Quoted in Carolyn E. Fick, 'The Saint-Domingue Slave Revolution and the Unfolding of Independence, 1791–1804', in David Patrick Geggus and Norman Fiering (eds), *The World of the Haitian Revolution* (Bloomington: Indiana University Press, 2009), p. 181.

45. Nick Nesbitt (ed.), *Toussaint Louverture* (London: Verso: 2008), p. 45.

46. 'Haitian Constitution of 1801' in Nesbitt (ed.), *Toussaint Louverture*, pp. 46, 48. The Constitution is also reproduced in Dubois and Garrigus, *Slave Revolution in the Caribbean*, pp. 167–70.

47. 'Haitian Constitution of 1801', p. 46.

48. 'Haitian Constitution of 1801', p. 48.
49. 'Haitian Constitution of 1801', p. 47.
50. 'Haitian Constitution of 1801', p. 47.
51. 'Haitian Constitution of 1801', p. 48.
52. 'Haitian Constitution of 1801', pp. 50–1.
53. 'Haitian Constitution of 1801', p. 59.
54. 'Haitian Constitution of 1801', p. 51.
55. Geggus, 'Toussaint Louverture and the Haitian Revolution', pp. 127–9.
56. Fick, 'The Saint-Domingue Slave Revolution and the Unfolding of Independence, 1791–1804', p. 184.
57. Toussaint Louverture, 'Letter to Napoleon on the 1801 Constitution', in Nesbitt (ed.), *Toussaint Louverture*, pp. 42–3.
58. Girard, *Toussaint Louverture*, p. 225.
59. Dubois, *Avengers of the New World*, pp. 246–7. Geggus, 'Toussaint Louverture and the Haitian Revolution', p. 128. On the prohibition of the whip and reduction in the length of the working day, see Korngold, *Citizen Toussaint*, p. 166.
60. Dubois, *Avengers of the New World*, p. 246.
61. Bell, *Toussaint Louverture*, p. 207; Rachel Beauvoir-Dominique, 'Moyse Hyacinthe Louverture (1773–1801)', in Franklin W. Knight and Henry Louis Gates Jr (eds), *Dictionary of Caribbean and Afro-Latin American Biography*, Vol. 4 (Oxford: Oxford University Press, 2016), p. 129. See the account by a white contemporary of the uprising in Geggus (ed.), *The Haitian Revolution*, pp. 164–5.
62. Dubois, *Avengers of the New World*, p. 247. Fick, *The Making of Haiti*, p. 210.
63. Toussaint Louverture, 'Proclamation', in Nesbitt (ed.), *Toussaint Louverture*, pp. 66–7.
64. Louverture, 'Proclamation', p. 67.
65. Louverture, 'Proclamation', p. 68.
66. Geggus (ed.), *The Haitian Revolution*, p. 166.
67. Dubois, *Avengers of the New World*, pp. 248–9.
68. Louverture, 'Proclamation', p. 70.
69. Louverture, 'Proclamation', p. 70.
70. Nesbitt (ed.), *Toussaint Louverture*, p. 65.
71. Dubois, *Avengers of the New World*, pp. 249–50.
72. V.G. Kiernan, 'Visionary and fighter', *Guardian*, 8 December 1978.
73. Frederick Engels, *The Peasant War in Germany* (Moscow: Progress, 1956), pp. 138–9.
74. See for example the brief but telling psychological portrait of Louverture from this period painted by Michel-Étienne Descourtilz, a white French captive from 1799–1802, in Popkin, *Facing Racial Revolution*, p. 277.
75. Geggus, 'Toussaint Louverture and the Haitian Revolution', p. 129.

76. James, *The Black Jacobins*, p. 144. For more on Robespierre, see George Rudé, *Robespierre: Portrait of a Revolutionary Democrat* (London: Collins, 1975).

77. James, *The Black Jacobins*, pp. 231–3.

78. See reference to the unsent letter Bonaparte wrote praising Louverture in 1801 before he heard about Santo Domingo and the Constitution in Girard, *Toussaint Louverture*, p. 230.

79. Fick, 'The Saint-Domingue Slave Revolution and the Unfolding of Independence, 1791–1804', p. 185.

80. James, *The Black Jacobins*, pp. 220–1.

81. For British representations of Louverture in this period, see Grégory Pierrot, '"Our Hero": Toussaint Louverture in British Representations', *Criticism*, 50, no. 4 (2008), pp. 581–607.

82. Girard, *Toussaint Louverture*, p. 234.

83. Girard, *Toussaint Louverture*, p. 166.

84. Bell, *Toussaint Louverture*, p. 197. James, *The Black Jacobins*, p. 213.

Chapter 5: The Harder They Come, The Harder They Fall ... : 1801–03

1. James, *The Black Jacobins*, p. 219.

2. See Philippe Girard, *The Slaves who Defeated Napoléon: Toussaint L'Ouverture and the Haitian War of Independence, 1801–1804* (Tuscaloosa: The University of Alabama Press, 2011) pp. 34–5.

3. James, *The Black Jacobins*, p. 223.

4. Cited in James, *The Black Jacobins*, p. 223.

5. James, *The Black Jacobins*, p. 224.

6. Girard, *The Slaves who Defeated Napoléon*, p. 62.

7. Cited in Geggus (ed.), *The Haitian Revolution*, p. 172.

8. Girard, *Toussaint Louverture*, p. 235.

9. Quoted by Popkin, *A Concise History of the Haitian Revolution*, p. 121.

10. James, *The Black Jacobins*, p. 241.

11. Cited in Nesbitt, *Toussaint Louverture*, p. 76.

12. James, *The Black Jacobins*, p. 243.

13. Cited in James, *The Black Jacobins*, pp. 245–6.

14. Girard, *Toussaint* Louverture, p. 238.

15. Cited by Popkin, *A Concise History of the Haitian Revolution*, p. 123.

16. On Sanité Belair, who featured in 2004 on a Haitian banknote, see James, *The Black Jacobins*, pp. 209, 280, 284.

17. James, *The Black Jacobins*, p. 248.

18. James, *The Black Jacobins*, p. 258.

19. Cited in Popkin, *A Concise History of the Haitian Revolution*, p. 125.

20. James, *The Black Jacobins*, p. 219. See also Tom Reiss, *The Black Count: Napoleon's Rival and the Real Count of Monte Cristo – General Alexandre Dumas* (London: Vintage Books, 2013).

21. Cited in Geggus, *The Haitian Revolution*, p. 173.

22. James, *The Black Jacobins*, p. 267. Girard notes of this encounter, 'French officers thronged inside to catch a glimpse of the famous Toussaint Louverture. One of them snickered that it was impossible "to obtain white flour from a sack of coal". Louverture stopped for a second, glanced at the officers assembled before him, and replied with a bon mot of his own: "Perhaps, but a sack of coal is enough to melt bronze".' Girard, *Toussaint Louverture*, p. 241.

23. Cited in Popkin, *A Concise History of the Haitian Revolution*, p. 129.

24. Bell, *Toussaint Louverture*, p. 264.

25. Cited in James, *The Black Jacobins*, p. 271.

26. Édouard Glissant, *Monsieur Toussaint: A Play*, trans. J. Michael Dash (Boulder, CO: Lynne Rienner, 2005).

27. Girard, *Toussaint Louverture*, p. 11.

28. Cited in Bell, *Toussaint Louverture*, p. 267.

29. Auguste Nemours, *Histoire de la captivité et de la mort de Toussaint Louverture. Notre pèlerinage au fort de Joux* (Nancy; Paris; Strasbourg: Berger-Levrault, 1929).

30. Cited in Bell, *Toussaint Louverture*, p. 268.

31. Charles Forsdick, 'Transatlantic displacement and the problematics of space', in Mary Gallagher (ed.), *Ici-Là: Place and Displacement in Caribbean Writing in French* (Amsterdam: Rodopi, 2003), pp. 181–209.

32. Derek Walcott, *What the Twilight Says* (New York: Farrar, Straus, and Giroux, 1998), p. 13.

33. James, *The Black Jacobins*, p. 293.

34. Girard, *Toussaint Louverture*, p. 251.

35. Philippe R. Girard (ed.), *The Memoir of General Toussaint Louverture* (Oxford: Oxford University Press, 2014), p. 53.

36. Girard (ed.), *The Memoir of General Toussaint Louverture*, pp. 23–30.

37. Girard (ed.), *The Memoir of General Toussaint Louverture*, p. 32.

38. Nemours, *Histoire de la captivité et de la mort de Toussaint Louverture*, p. 110.

39. James, *The Black Jacobins*, p. 294.

40. James, *The Black Jacobins*, p. 271.

41. James, *The Black Jacobins*, p. 291.

42. For numbers of lives lost, see Philippe Girard, 'Liberté, Égalité, Esclavage: French Revolutionary Ideals and the Failure of the Leclerc Expedition to Saint-Domingue', *French Colonial History*, 6 (2005), 55–77.

43. Cited in James, *The Black Jacobins*, p. 300.

44. Girard, *Toussaint Louverture*, p. 255.

45. Robin Blackburn, *The American Crucible: Slavery, Emancipation and Human Rights* (London: Verso, 2011), p. 175.

46. Blackburn, *The American Crucible*, p. 198.

Chapter 6: . . . One and All: 1804–

1. David Geggus, 'The Caribbean in the Age of Revolution', in David Armitage and Sanjoy Subrahmanyam (eds), *The Age of Revolutions in Global Context, c.1760–1840* (Basingstoke: Palgrave Macmillan, 2010), p. 85.

2. Geggus, 'The Caribbean in the Age of Revolution', pp. 85, 89, 91. See also Blackburn, *The Overthrow of Colonial Slavery*; Gelian Matthews, *Caribbean Slave Revolts and the British Abolitionist Movement* (Baton Rouge: Louisiana State University Press, 2006), and David P. Geggus (ed.), *The Impact of the Haitian Revolution in the Atlantic World* (Columbia: University of South Carolina Press, 2001).

3. Craton, *Testing the Chains*, pp. 335–9.

4. Craton, *Testing the Chains*, p. 236.

5. Ada Ferrer, 'Speaking of Haiti: Slavery, Revolution, and Freedom in Cuban Slave Testimony', in David Patrick Geggus and Norman Fiering (eds), *The World of the Haitian Revolution* (Bloomington: Indiana University Press, 2009), pp. 235, 237.

6. Craton, *Testing the Chains*, p. 261.

7. Geggus, 'The Caribbean in the Age of Revolution', p. 85.

8. Samuel Warner, 'Authentic and Impartial Narrative of the Tragical Scene…', in Henry Irving Tragle, *The Southampton Slave Revolt of 1831: A Compilation of Source Material* (Amherst: The University of Massachusetts Press, 1971), p. 282.

9. Matthew J. Clavin, 'American Toussaints: Symbol, Subversion, and the Black Atlantic Tradition in the American Civil War', *Slavery and Abolition*, 28, no. 1 (2007), p. 91.

10. David Geggus, 'British Opinion and the Emergence of Haiti, 1791–1805', in James Walvin (ed.), *Slavery and British Society 1776–1846* (London: Macmillan, 1982), p. 136.

11. James, *The Black Jacobins*, p. 321. In fact, there were six states: Bolivia, Colombia, Ecuador, Panama, Peru and Venezuela. In return Bolívar promised to end slavery in the lands he liberated. See Blackburn, *The American Crucible*, p. 175.

12. Kevin Whelan, 'The Green Atlantic: radical reciprocities between Ireland and America in the long eighteenth century', in Kathleen Wilson (ed.), *A New Imperial History: Culture, Identity and Modernity in Britain and the Empire, 1660–1840* (Cambridge: Cambridge University Press, 2004), pp. 232, 234.

13. Marcus Rediker and Peter Linebaugh, *The Many-Headed Hydra: The Hidden History of the Revolutionary Atlantic* (London: Verso, 2000), p. 279. Rediker and Linebaugh cite here: Charles Vane (ed.), *Memoirs and Correspondence of Viscount Castlereagh*, Vol. II (London: Henry Colburn, 1848), p. 417.

14. Whelan, 'The Green Atlantic', pp. 233–5.

15. Geggus, 'British Opinion and the Emergence of Haiti, 1791–1805', pp. 137, 140, 144. As Cobbett put it: 'The Negroes are a bloody-minded race … they are made and marked for servitude and subjection; it is the purpose which they were obviously intended for.'

16. Cited in Tyson, *Toussaint L'Ouverture*, p. 110.

17. Cited in Tyson, *Toussaint L'Ouverture*, pp. 122–3.

18. Hazel Waters, *Racism on the Victorian Stage: Representation of Slavery and the Black Character* (Cambridge: Cambridge University Press, 2007), pp. 118, 122, 190, 214.

19. James, *The Black Jacobins*, p. 336. For a similar portrait of Louverture's 'virtuous character' published in Leeds, England in 1848, see Wilson Armistead, *A Tribute for the Negro* (Miami, FL: Mnemosyne, 1969), pp. 267–307.

20. Quoted in Matthew J. Clavin, *Toussaint Louverture and the American Civil War: The Promise and Peril of a Second Haitian Revolution* (Philadelphia: University of Pennsylvania Press, 2010), p. 1. Du Bois had himself recognised the importance of Toussaint in his 1896 doctoral dissertation, and he hailed 'Toussaint the Saviour' in his classic text *The Souls of Black Folk* (1903). See W.E.B. Du Bois, *The Souls of Black Folk* (New York: Dover Publications, 1994), p. 31. For Du Bois's later reflections, see W.E.B. Du Bois, 'Toussaint L'Ouverture' [1961], in Eric J. Sundquist (ed.), *The Oxford W.E.B. Du Bois Reader* (Oxford: Oxford University Press, 1996), pp. 296–302.

21. Clavin, *Toussaint Louverture and the American Civil War*, p. 5.

22. Cited by Tyson, *Toussaint L'Ouverture*, p. 129.

23. Cited by Tyson, *Toussaint L'Ouverture*, p. 142.

24. Cited by Tyson, *Toussaint L'Ouverture*, p. 140.

25. Frederick Douglass, 'Lecture on Haiti', in Maurice Jackson and Jacqueline Baker (eds), *African Americans and the Haitian Revolution* (New York, Routledge, 2010), pp. 202–10 (p. 209).

26. *Daily Gleaner*, 10 October 1893; W. Adolphe Roberts, *Six Great Jamaicans* (Kingston: Pioneer Press, 1957), p. 77, quoted in Matthew J. Smith, '"To Place Ourselves in History": The Haitian Revolution in British West Indian Thought before *The Black Jacobins*', in Charles Forsdick and Christian Høgsbjerg (eds), *The Black Jacobins Reader* (Durham, NC: Duke University Press, 2017), p. 184.

27. *Daily Gleaner*, 12 October 1893, quoted in Smith, "To Place Ourselves in History", p. 185.

28. *Daily Gleaner*, 2 August 1929, quoted in Smith, "'To Place Ourselves in History'", pp. 185–6.

29. Ian H. Birchall, *The Spectre of Babeuf* (Basingstoke: Macmillan, 1997), p. 136.

30. Peter Fryer, *Staying Power: A History of Black People in Britain* (London: Pluto Press, 1984), p. 211.

31. See Hassan Mahamdallie, *Black British Radicals: Figures from Working Class History* (London: Bookmarks, 2012) and Michael Morris, "Robert Wedderburn: race, religion and revolution", *International Socialism*, 132 (2011), pp. 130-162. Wedderburn, in *The Axe Laid to the Root or A Fatal Blow to Oppressors, Being an Address to the Planters and Negroes of the Island of Jamaica* (1817), noted a prediction that 'Jamaica will be in the hands of the blacks within twenty years', and wrote 'Prepare for flight, ye planters, for the fate of St. Domingo awaits you . . . Recollect the fermentation will be universal'. See Iain MacCalman (ed.), *The Horrors of Slavery and other writings by Robert Wedderburn* (Edinburgh: Edinburgh University Press, 1991), p. 86.

32. Betty Fladeland, "Our Cause being One and the Same': Abolitionists and Chartism', in James Walvin (ed.), *Slavery and British Society 1776–1846* (London: Macmillan, 1982), p. 99.

33. Karl Marx, *Capital*, Vol. I (Harmondsworth: Penguin, 1976), p. 414.

34. Cyril Briggs, 'Negro Revolutionary Hero – Toussaint L'Ouverture', *The Communist*, 8, no. 5 (May 1929). On the US occupation of Haiti, see Raphael Dalleo, *American Imperialism's Undead: The Occupation of Haiti and the Rise of Caribbean Anticolonialism* (Charlottesville: University of Virginia Press, 2016).

35. George Padmore, 'A Wave of Terror is Sweeping over Haiti', *Negro Worker* (February–March 1933), quoted in Dalleo, *American Imperialism's Undead*, p. 38.

36. For more on this, see Christian Høgsbjerg, 'C.L.R. James and Italy's Conquest of Abyssinia', *Socialist History*, 28 (2006).

37. See 'A London Diary,' *New Statesman*, 3 August 1935. See also the *News Chronicle*, 29 July 1935, online at www.ourmigrationstory.org.uk/uploads/hogsbjerg_international%20friends%20of%20ethiopia.pdf.

38. See Charles Forsdick and Christian Høgsbjerg, 'Sergei Eisenstein and the Haitian Revolution: "The Confrontation Between Black and White Explodes into Red"', *History Workshop Journal*, 78 (2014), pp. 157–85.

39. Philip Foner (ed.) *Paul Robeson Speaks* (Secaucas, NJ: Citadel Press, 1978), pp. 377–9.

40. James, *The Black Jacobins*, pp. 305, 308.

41. James, *The Black Jacobins*, p. 196.
42. Geggus, 'The Caribbean in the Age of Revolution', p. 97.
43. Girard, *Toussaint Louverture*, p. 209.
44. Frederick Engels, 'On Authority' (1872), www.marxists.org/archive/marx/works/1872/10/authority.htm
45. James, *The Black Jacobins*, pp. 200–1.
46. James, *The Black Jacobins*, p. 230.
47. John Agard, 'Toussaint L'Ouverture acknowledges Wordsworth's sonnet "To Toussaint L'Ouverture"', in *Half-caste and Other Poems* (London: Hodder, 2004), p. 63.
48. Barrington Braithwaite, *Drums of Freedom: The Saga of the Haitian Revolution* (New York: Davie Press, 2015).
49. *Jacobin*, a quarterly magazine based in New York, presents itself as the 'leading voice of the American left, offering socialist perspectives on politics, economics, and culture'. The logo and branding of the publication were inspired by James's *The Black Jacobins*.
50. Gina Athena Ulysse *Why Haiti Needs New Narratives: A Post-Quake Chronicle* (Middletown, CT: Wesleyan University Press, 2015).
51. Paul Foot, 'Toussaint L'Ouverture: The Haitian Slave Revolt of 1791' (1991) www.marxists.org/archive/foot-paul/1991/07/toussaint.html.
52. C.L.R. James, 'Revolution and the Negro', in Scott McLemee and Paul Le Blanc (eds), *C.L.R. James and Revolutionary Marxism: Selected Writings of C.L.R. James, 1939–49* (New York: Humanity Books, 2000), p. 77; Paul Foot, 'The Black Jacobin', *New Statesman*, 2 February 1979.
53. Girard, *Toussaint Louverture*, p. 2.
54. James, *The Black Jacobins*, p. 208.

Index